The Killer & I

A Journal About the Making
of Kane Hodder's
Biography, *Unmasked*

By
Michael Aloisi

www.AuthorMikeInk.com

ISBN: 0-9845801-8-2
ISBN-13: 978-0-9845801-8-7
Library of Congress Control Number: 2011911770

First Published by *AuthorMike Dark Ink*, 10/01/2011

www.AuthorMikeInk.com

AuthorMike Ink, *AuthorMike Dark Ink* and its logos are trademarked by *AuthorMike Ink Publishing*.

Printed in the United States of America

This book should be dedicated to Kane Hodder.
It is about him after all. Since he has cut about
ten years off my life from scaring me repeatedly,
I don't want to dedicate it to him.
So this book is *not* dedicated to Kane Hodder.

NOTE TO THE READER

When I started this journal, I had no intentions of ever releasing this as a book. It was due to the overwhelming response from its readers and Kane's fans that this is being published. And for that I am extremely grateful and thank all of you for reading and supporting Kane and myself through this crazy adventure.

With that said, since this was originally meant as a personal journal to document my own life and give occasional updates to the fans, it is not written with the best of prose. If I had known that it would be released as a book and not just kept as my own personal file of the time I spent with the man who terrified my childhood, I might have put a lot more detail into it. Regardless, I still think it's a fun read and that you will enjoy hearing the stories how Kane terrified me on a daily basis!

This journal was written as the events took place in my life. Meaning, you'll get to see how things changed during the process; everything from the title to the release date and more. You'll get to see how excited I was for upcoming events and even read the updates about things we were working on at the time.

If you have a keen eye, you might also note how the writing changes throughout. From sparse, quick entries updating the fans to longer stories as the journal became more fun to write.

If you want to read some of my more polished writing, make sure to check out Kane's biography, *Unmasked.* And be sure to be on the lookout for new journal updates of Kane and my adventures as we head out on the road in *The Killer and I: On the Road…to Hell.*

*You might have noticed the asterisk on the Cover Title. Kane made me put it there to let people know that the Book Title is grammatically incorrect. While that is true, I created the title as a play on the classic Broadway Show, *The King and I.* So for all you grammar nuts out there, we know it is wrong, so deal with it.

-AuthorMike

INTRODUCTION

When I was around ten years old, my father built me and my brother a fort in our backyard. We wanted a tree fort, but my father was always worried about us getting hurt, so we got a top of the line clubhouse. In reality it was a nice shed converted to a fort. It had windows that opened and a door with a lock and everything. My brother Jason and I quickly filled it up with stuff, including a carpet, beanbag chairs, toys and posters. For two young boys, it was a palace. No other kid around had anything similar; it was great.

Word quickly got around about our amazing fort and so called "friends" from all the neighboring streets started dropping by, wanting to hang out. Jason was three years older than me and had friends even older than him... teenage friends. Of course being older, wiser and tougher, these kids bullied their way into our fort. Being the young one, I played outside while the big boys hung out inside of it. One day after they left, I raced inside, excited to finally be able to hang out in *my* fort. Bursting through the door I was excited to play with my favorite Inspector Gadget doll I had stored in my secret box. Just as I took one step towards it, I froze in fear. I felt my tiny heart start to race, my bladder got weak and wanted to let go of itself… and I started to cry.

Without being able to get my favorite toy, I ran out of the fort, across the yard and into my house screaming. My parents were not home, we were being babysat by my Meme and Pepe. I didn't want them to see me crying, so I snuck into my room and shut the door. Once safely inside, with my two dozen Pound Purries (yes, I had a collection of stuffed cat dolls), I tried to stop crying, but the image that frightened me was still in my mind… I couldn't get it out. The man with the hockey mask was just… just so damn scary.

When I settled down that day I went to my brother and asked him to take the picture of the scary man down. He tried to reassure me it was just a picture, that it couldn't hurt me, besides *Jason Voorhees is not real*, he said. He'd ask his friend to take it down later, but he didn't want to take it down yet, because the guy who put it up was one of the cool kids and he didn't want him to think he was a dork for taking it down. I protested that I would tell Mom and Dad, but that just got me a punch in the arm.

For the next two weeks I stayed far, far away from the clubhouse. I couldn't and wouldn't go in there with that frightening man staring at me. Even if he was standing in Times Square, he scared me. I was so petrified of this man in a hockey mask that I couldn't get within twenty yards of the fort. I started having nightmares about him. My parents would run into my room in the middle of the night to assure me, everything was all right. There was no man with a mask who was going to hurt me.

The Clubhouse My Dad Built

With a stroke of some horrible timing, that very week I was scared of the hockey mask guy, my parents took Jason and I to the Big E, New England's largest fair. We loved the fair more than anything and looked forward to it every year, especially the mid-way. We loved the rides, house of mirrors, the food and of course the games. The one thing I stayed away from was the haunted houses. Though this year, when I saw the girl I liked from school go into one, I let my brother talk me into going through it. I was more than petrified, but the fact that a girl my age could do

5

it meant I could, no, had to as well. Staying as close to my brother as I could, I walked through the dark doorway and into the tunnel. My adolescent brain has blocked out most of the horrors I endured during that fateful walk through the haunted house, especially the part where I lost my brother and was on my own. Groups of teenagers pushed their way past the little boy clutching the wall for safety. The only part I remember with any clarity... was the exit, which was blocked by none other than... Jason Voorhees.

The second I walked around the corner and saw the big man standing there with a hockey mask on his face and a chainsaw in his hands, I fell to the floor. I was so scared I wouldn't walk by him, even though the exit was inches behind. I quickly crawled behind the corner and cried. Dozens of people kept walking past me laughing; a few teens even kicked me on the side. Yet I wouldn't budge. I couldn't. I had never been so scared in my life. All I could hear was the chainsaw revving and kids screaming. It was my worst nightmare. I was going to die and all because I wanted to show a girl I was cool.

After a few moments, no one was walking by me; I was alone with Jason. I dared a peek up, only to see he was coming near me. This was it; this was the end of my life. Then, suddenly, the chainsaw stopped. I looked up to see Jason was coming at me. That was when the screams started to come out of me.

"For Christ sake kid, just go!" Looking up I saw that the monster had removed his mask... it was just a teenager, not a monster.

"Hurry up before someone else comes." Taking the opportunity, I ran by him as fast as I could and into the arms of my concerned mother outside. I didn't care if the girl I liked saw me, I was safe. The nightmares were horrible that night and for the next few weeks. After that night I finally told my parents about the picture. They made my brother take it down and punished him. While Jason Voorhees still haunted my dreams, at least I could go into my fort now.

Flash forward three years to the summer of my thirteenth birthday. I was not your normal young teenage boy. I didn't listen to Pearl Jam or Nirvana, work out and watch horror movies like most of my friends did. Instead I listened to Weird Al Yankovic, baked cookies on a weekly basis and still collected my Pound Purries. Horror movies to me were evil. I had never seen one and never wanted to. The thought of watching one made my stomach turn and my adolescent bladder expel pee. I'm not sure why I thought horror movies were so... horrible for a lack of better words. It could have been that my mom hated them, but it's probably due to the fact that I was just plain scared of them.

I vividly remember when all of that changed. It was a typical day hanging out at my friend Mike's house. We swam, he made me listen to a band that did not make me laugh and we ate junk food. In the afternoon we got bored and asked his mom to take us to the video store to rent a movie. She obliged and we were quickly whisked away to the dingy old store searching the aisles. Of course I picked up my favorites like Police Academy, Weird Science and Howard the Duck. I had seen them all a million times, but wanted to see them again. Mike on the other hand was in the aisle I had never walked down, the one that I always watched out of the corner of my eye as if it might jump out and attack me... the horror section. Without even asking me, he grabbed a movie and handed it to his mother who walked to the checkout counter. I looked at the armful of movies I had, wishing he would pick one of these, but it was too late.

Back at his house I tried to make an excuse that I had to leave, that I wasn't feeling well and I had forgotten that I had homework to do (even though it was summer break). Nothing worked; he wouldn't let me leave. In his den, he shut the curtains, closed the door and popped the movie into the VCR. I sat as far away from the screen as I could, grabbed a pillow and hugged it, terrified, knowing I would have weeks of nightmares to come. When I heard the creepy, yet oddly goofy music I looked up to see giant words flying at the screen. *What... what was this movie?* I asked in a whisper.

"It's a Jason movie..." I believe I might have fainted at this point. When I awoke, I dared a peek through my fingers. *Friday the 13th Part 3... in 3D!* The title yelled at me. I was glad we didn't have the glasses. After closing my eyes for the first kill I dared to look at the second one. Oddly, I laughed a bit. Curious, I got off of the couch and joined my friend on the ground, still keeping the pillow for safety. Then, there was another kill and the oddest thing happened… we both laughed. When I saw a set of glorious breasts, my sexually forming mind threw the pillow behind me and started to pay attention. This movie was sort of… fun.

Honestly, I can say that day changed my life. For the first time, I had enjoyed horror. I wasn't scared of it; it was fun! When I went home that night I proudly told my mother that I had watched a horror movie, and that it wasn't scary. She wasn't too thrilled that her thirteen year old was allowed to watch boobs and gore, but she nodded and told me she was proud of me for not being scared, but that I shouldn't be watching them.

With another stroke of coincidence, that August happened to have a Friday the 13th in it. Flipping through the channels, I found that USA was having a *Friday the 13th* movie marathon. With my newfound confidence of watching horror movies, I plunked myself down and watched Parts 7 and 8, three times that weekend. The films blew my mind. This Jason guy was fierce and mean. He killed people over and over again and yet I found myself rooting for him. From that weekend on, I was addicted to horror and *Friday the 13th* was my drug of choice.

A couple of months later, being hooked on the genre, I found out that the new *Friday the 13th* was on Pay-Per-View. I waited until my parents went to bed and snuck down to the basement. Quietly as I could I picked up the phone and ordered the movie. A grounding for ordering a movie, especially an R rated movie, was in my future, but it was worth the risk. Shutting off the lights I laid down in my beanbag and put the TV on the right channel. Laying there I suddenly felt the all too familiar nerves creep into my body. Maybe I wasn't ready for this. All the other movies I had watched during the day, upstairs, where it was bright. My heart raced. I could do this.

When Jason showed up on the screen for the first time, I lost my breath; he looked scarier than ever before. Amazingly, I got through the movie and snuck back into my bedroom upstairs. As I hugged my favorite Pound Purrie, I thought about Jason Voorhees. He was so cool, so badass. I started to wonder about the guy who played him, was he really that tough in real life? Was he mean? What was his name? Kane, it was Kane something. I remember seeing it on several of the movies. He had to be pretty damn cool... I'd never want to meet him though. He was probably scary in real life.

As I grew up and became obsessed with horror movies, Kane slowly but surely became a God like legend in my eyes. My entire bedroom was decorated in horror posters and paraphernalia. During my high school years (sadly during the eight year draught when there were no *Friday the 13ᵗʰ* films) I had a teacher who was a huge horror fan, he even wrote for a small horror magazine. Of course, this teacher quickly became the coolest person in the world to me. One particular Monday in class, I remember crowding around his desk as he showed us pictures from a convention he went to... a horror convention. The picture he was most proud of was of Kane Hodder choking him! He went on and on about how cool Kane was, how he really choked him and that he couldn't believe he met Jason Voorhees. At that age, I couldn't imagine ever meeting a celebrity; it just seemed like something that would never happen to a small town kid. Even though I never thought it would happen, I told myself that someday... I would meet Kane Hodder.

My Favorite Pound Purrie, Patches

Right after my twentieth birthday, one of the greatest days of my life happened; there was finally going to be a *Friday the 13th* film released in the theaters! *Jason X.* I don't know if it was the fact that it was the first film in the franchise I could actually see in the theaters, but I loved it. I went to the ten in the morning showing on the first day it came out and then saw it again two more times that day. Getting to see Jason on the big screen, especially Kane Hodder's Jason, was amazing. Sadly, it was the only time I would ever get to experience that.

Almost ten years later, still a huge horror fan, I found out that there would be a horror convention only an hour away from my house. I had never been to one. The idea of going and getting to meet celebrities I grew up watching, was overwhelming. My wife, who hates horror, graciously accompanied me and let me spend a small fortune getting autographs in the bible (also known as *Crystal Lake Memories*). I met Robert Englund, Bruce Campbell and five of the guys who played Jason Voorhees. My giddiness would have surpassed any ten year old at Disney World. I was jumping up and down, grabbing my wife's arm every few seconds and whispering in here ear: *Oh my god, its Nancy from Nightmare, look Derek Mears, holy crap it's the dude from Roger Rabbit (why is he here?), oh, oh, oh, look there is Bruce Campbell!* I was going nuts.

Exhausted and completely broke, I hugged the bible to my chest and turned to my wife as we were ready to leave and said, *If I could just meet Kane Hodder… my life would be complete. If I could get him to sign my book, I, I don't know what I would do.* Of course she asked me who he was and I had to stop and explain his God-like status to her. She smiled and said that was nice and I'd probably get to meet him at a convention one day.

Little did I know that a year later, my life would revolve around the man that I was infatuated with my entire life. That is what this journal is about, my year-long adventure with the monster that terrified my childhood and hung on my walls during my teen (fine… and adult) life. I could never have imagined that I would be talking to Kane Hodder on a daily basis, visiting him on movie sets, hanging out with him at conventions, going on ghost hunts with him and more than that, I could have never, ever guessed that he would scare me a hell of a lot more now that we were friends than he ever did when I was a child.

This is… *The Killer and I*

Michael Aloisi

A KILLER CALL

It was just shy of ten at night when the phone rang. No one ever called me that late so I gave my wife a curious look.

"Probably a telemarketer," she said as I looked at the number. *Unlisted.* Usually I don't answer unlisted numbers, but for some reason I picked it up. Of course, not wanting to talk to a telemarketer I answered in a deep voice so I could disguise it and say that Michael wasn't home (not like they would know how my voice sounded anyway). I answered with a gurgled *hello*, ready to blow off the caller who was probably going to want me to donate money to save orphaned cats in Ireland or to check my credit score seven hundred times a day for only five-hundred dollars a month.

"Hello, Mike? This is Kane Hodder." I let out a quick laugh, Kane Hodder, right. Who was playing a trick on me? My brother? Friend? I was ready to call them out when I suddenly remembered that I emailed him two weeks earlier…. Realizing this wasn't a joke, I jumped off of my couch, and replied with,

"Kane Hodder, Kane Hodder is calling me…okay, okay, hello!" My wife, knowing my obsession with him, jumped up as well and covered her mouth to hold in a giddy scream. In a panic, I ran to my office and turned on my computer to pull up whatever information I needed to sound professional and prepared, like I normally was.

I paced back and forth as we started to chat about the email I had sent him. A few weeks earlier, I took a break from the daily running's of my publishing company that I had just launched. Being a huge horror movie fan, I decided to watch something gory during my break. Being a big fan of Kane's, I picked *Ed Gein: The Butcher of Plainfield*. As I watched it, I thought about how interesting of a life Kane had. I was curious if he had a biography out, for I'd love to read about his life. After doing a few searches, I found out that he didn't have a book. I was a bit disappointed by this, but then realized that *I* could be the one to write it. Over the next few hours I worked up a proposal for a book about his life, found his contact information and sent the email. It would be a dream job and I knew it was a long shot, so I really didn't think much of it after that moment...until that phone call that is.

For a solid twenty minutes I paced back and forth, rambling and stumbling my way through our conversation as my wife watched me with a notepad in hand. Kane liked my ideas, but he needed some time to think about my proposal. He agreed to call me back in a few days, and with that we said our good byes. As I hung up the phone, I promptly fell to the floor and started to yell with excitement. My wife laughed and joined in with my celebratory yells before helping me get up. As I got up, my Jason Voorhees figurine on my bookshelf caught my eye...*Jesus, I just talked to him.*

After doing a dance of joy, I called a few of my horror movie buddies and my brother to tell them I just talked to Kane F'ing Hodder! I couldn't believe it, just a few months before this phone call, my wife and I went to a horror convention and met five of the guys who played Jason Voorhees. I got them all to sign my copy of *Crystal Lake Memories*. When we left, I turned to my wife and said, "If I could just meet Kane Hodder, my life would be complete." Now he was calling *me* to talk about writing a book together! That night, when I went to bed, I said I thought to myself that even if he decided not to do the book, at least I got to talk to one of my idols.

The next several days as I worked on other book projects, I kept the phone glued to my hands, waiting for Kane to call back....

Michael Aloisi

A KILLER ON MY MIND

The days after Kane's phone call were tense. The prospect of writing a book about a horror legend consumed my thoughts. All day I walked around like a zombie, thinking about how I'd approach the writing of the book, what style would I put it in, how would I market it and most importantly, how to make sure it pleased his fans and other readers alike.

For days I wrote down notes, plotted out the book and researched Kane all I could to be prepared for the next time he called. I watched movie after movie that he was in, searched for interviews and clips of Kane's online and even read Robert Englund's biography to have a similar book to compare to the one I had proposed. The next time Kane called, I was ready, sort of.

The call came one afternoon as I was working on some paper work in my office. Though I had prepared for days, I started to lose my breath when I heard the voice on the line say "Hey Mike, it's Kane Hodder". I still just couldn't believe Kane was calling me. We chatted a bit (as I paced back and forth in my office instead sitting at my desk like I normally did for business calls) as I did my best to prove to him that why I was the one to write his book.

Kane understandably had some concerns and I did my best to answer every question honestly. Come to find out, he had been thinking about writing a book for years, even had many offers, but he just hadn't found the right place yet. That is why I guaranteed him that we wouldn't put the book out until he was 100% satisfied with it. The vision would be exactly what he wanted and that he would have final approval of the manuscript and the cover (something almost never done in publishing). He liked everything I said, but still needed more time. I understood this, but it meant I had to wait more

Over the next few weeks we talked a few times and I emailed him random thoughts here and there about my vision for the book. I was getting more comfortable talking with him and felt confident we worked well together, which is important, being that we would have to work together for over a year on this project.

Then, one day I was driving home and my cell rang…it was Kane, he was just leaving Comic Con after promoting *Hatchet 2*. We talked about the convention for a bit, but then got down to business. He asked a few more questions, but then, just as I was about to pull into my driveway, Kane said, "All right, let's do this." I had to hold in a scream to act professional.

When I hung up the phone I noticed I was stopped in the middle of my street; I hadn't even pulled into the driveway. As I tried to catch my breath, my wife just happened to drive down the street. Seeing me, she slowed down to try and figure out why I was in the middle of the road. Instead of pulling into the driveway, I jumped out of my car and danced in the road. Amazingly, my wife instantly knew why I was dancing...I had just signed a "killer" client to my company.

FRIDAY THE 13ᵗʰ… THE CONTRACT

Kane had officially agreed to have Dark Ink and myself write and publish his book. All that was left to do was to sign the contracts and get started on the book. Of course, like with any contracts, they get sent back and forth between both parties until they are agreed upon. This process went really well with Kane and I as we quickly agreed upon the contract terms. When we were both ready to sign, I realized that a certain date just happened to be coming up in two weeks…Friday the 13ᵗʰ.

Though I was eager to get the contracts signed and start on the book, I couldn't help but think about how cool it would be to sign the contracts on that day. I shot an email about the idea to Kane and he loved it. There has always been a strong link to the number 13 in his life, not only because of the movies (you can read all about that in the book!). With that, a deal was made; we were to both sign the official contracts, on the date that made him famous.

When the 13ᵗʰ arrived we both signed the contracts and set the book into production. There was an eerie, yet exciting feeling signing the contract on the 13ᵗʰ. Most people believe that day and number is bad luck. Some people even take it so seriously they don't go out of their house on that date, yet for Kane, fans of the franchise and myself, there couldn't be a better day. Especially since the *next* Friday the 13th, the only one of 2011, will see the release of *Kill!*

JASON VOORHEES INVITES ME TO A LAKE

"Jason Voorhees invites you to a lake and you say yes…are you f*cking nuts!" My brother cackled through the phone. The fact that Kane invited me to a lake in the woods never occurred to me. It was a creepy thought, but it made me more excited. Kane was scheduled to do a ghost hunt (more on Kane's ghost hunting later) in Lake George NY, only a few hours from my offices, so we decided to meet there to start on our book.

In the week before, I did all the research on Kane I could. I watched and read interviews online, re-watched as many of his films as I could and read several books. I felt prepared, only problem was, I was having eye surgery two days before I was to meet with Kane (PRK, similar to Lasik but with a longer healing time)! The surgery went well, but it left my vision…blurry to say the least. It was so blurry in fact, I couldn't drive myself up; my wife had to drive me. I was worried about what sort of impression I would first make, having to blink constantly and put drops in every five minutes, but I had no choice, I had to go.

When we arrived at the lake, a picturesque lake that many camp councilors probably work at, my wife

23

checked me into the hotel and helped me bring my stuff to my room (being that I had a hard time reading the room numbers). It was around eleven in the morning by the time I was in my room, ready to call Kane. I looked at the phone, nervous to call him even though I had already talked to him a dozen times on the phone. I was ready to start the interview process and to start working on the book, but I couldn't help but be nervous about meeting the man that haunted my childhood nightmares.

With a few deep breaths I finally called Kane. He said he would meet me in the lobby in forty-five minutes. Hanging up the phone I hated the fact that I had to sit and be nervous for almost another hour. To "kill" time, my wife and I walked the grounds of the beautiful hotel before heading to the lobby to wait. As I sat down on a fluffy chair, I checked my bag a few hundred times to make sure I had everything: computer, charger, note pad, pens, digital recorder and of course…eye drops.

For almost twenty minutes I stared at the elevator, squinting and staring at each person that walked out, waiting for Kane. After putting a few more eye drops in…I saw a large figure wearing a black shirt walk out of the elevator. It was him and it was time to meet the killer.

KANE BREAKS THE ICE

I have met countless celebrities in my life (or at least ran into them). Living in NYC for years, being an actor and doing all sorts of events I have run into everyone from Tom Cruise to Julia Roberts. Not once had I been nervous meeting these stars. It might have been the fact that a lot of the time I wasn't expecting to run into them. Yet, for some reason, before meeting Kane Hodder, I felt like I was going to throw up.

Walking across the hotel lobby I took deep breaths as I rubbed my eyes one more time in the hopes that I could see him clearly. About ten feet away I put on my best game face and stuck out my hand,

"Kane, Mike Aloisi, nice to finally meet you." He was wearing his trademark gloves, an energy drink was in one hand and he proudly wore his *Hatchet 2* shirt. As he crushed my hand with an enthusiastic shake, I could tell I was blushing and smiling a bit too big, like a nervous five-year-old meeting Mickey Mouse. My wife showed up behind me, smiling like the mother of the five-year-old, happy their child is seeing their hero. I awkwardly introduced her before pushing her off saying she had to go; this was business after all, I had to be professional. With that, Kane led the way outside. The hotel was going to let

25

us use their banquet hall so we'd have a private place to talk. The facilities were in their restaurant, in another building on the property.

On the walk over I did my best to not sweat or lose my breath from excitement as we chatted. This was my first impression; I had to be on my game. I kept telling myself to relax. I have had no problem working with any of my other clients, heck, I had fifteen books in production and written many of my own. Writing was my profession after all, and that was what I was here for, to write his book. I just had to be me. By the time we got settled into the banquet room, I was feeling a bit more comfortable, still nervous, but I was handling myself better. Our conversation was going well and Kane was being extremely cooperative and friendly, and I could tell he was going to be easy to work with.

After a couple hours of Kane telling me about his life, we took a break. I was feeling better and becoming more like myself, but having to put drops in my blurry eyes every five minutes made me feel awkward and embarrassed. I decided to go the bathroom to splash some water on my face to cool my eyes. The water refreshed me a bit, but I could still hardly see. Looking in the mirror I smiled at my hazy image, I could do this… I was doing this. After drying my face I walked out to the dark hallway. The restaurant didn't open until the evening so Kane and I were the only two people in there. Just as I put my hand on the door handle for the conference room, I heard a viscous, roaring, barking noise coming from my left.

Instantly, my heart leapt along with the rest of my body. As I turned, I saw a giant figure diving out at me from the black stairway, my obscured vision making this an even scarier image. As I let out a yelp, I realized it was, of course, Kane. Normally, I don't yell out loud and jump when someone tries to scare me, but this…I was not expecting.

After laughing and holding my chest for a few minutes (I think I might have had a mild heart attack), we went back into the room. My eyes might still have been blurry, my chest aching…but the ice had been broken. Seeing Kane's sense of humor and his passion for frightening people made me realize that I didn't need to be nervous around him. From that point on I have been able to relax and work with him at ease. And now, I can say that Jason Voorhees had scared the piss out of me in person!

THE TRUTH HURTS

The first meeting with Kane was long, exhaustive and more than amazing. Over the years I have read dozens of bio's on Kane. I realized during our talks that none of them were correct. Tiny snippets online are true, but there is hardly any of the real interesting stuff about his life online. His real story is fascinating, to say the least.

Most people's childhoods are average...ordinary. Kane's on the other hand, is the complete opposite. He grew up on a small tropical island...a really, really small island. How small? Only three miles long and a half-mile wide. Think about it, that is a fraction the size of most towns. Imagine never being able to leave a small section of where you live.

There was so much more I learned about Kane that day, things I never would have imagined or thought of...the most horrific though, was the truth behind the fire stunt that went horribly wrong. There are numerous stories on the Internet about how Kane got burned over 50% of his body, and not one of them is true. Kane opened up and told me the truth behind the burn... the true story that almost no one knows. Watching him tell me every detail of the incident that left him scarred for life, seeing the pain behind his

28

eyes and knowing that he was letting all out, made me realize that he was going to give this book everything he had.

Hearing Kane talk about how he watched his skin just fall right off his arms, how he was in the hospital for almost a year, suffering through ill-fated procedures, was scarier than any horror movie he ever starred in. Kane's burn and recovery in and of itself are riveting and heart wrenching enough to fill an entire book...and that happened at the beginning of his career.

THE WORK BEGINS

After our first meeting I went home and started doing more research. Kane had given me a ton of information, but I needed to fill some holes and refresh my memory on his movies. I did extensive research about the island he grew up on, studied burn victims and procedures for recovery to get a full understanding of the horror he went through, and most of all, watched a lot of his movies.

With over a hundred film credits to his name, I have hardly made a dent in the list. Everything from Chuck Norris and Steven Segal films to Oscar nominated movies like Monster are on my list. I have to research the stunts he did in hundreds of movies and shows. I need to see the stunts and watch them over and over again to get the colors and look to match the feelings that Kane told me he felt during them...otherwise they won't translate to the page.

The work is exhaustive and though I'm not with Kane most days, I find myself always "with" Kane whether it be watching one of his movies, researching his life or writing about it. At first I was a bit worried about getting tired of studying and writing about the same man for so long, but I haven't yet. And the reason for that is Kane's life is so interesting that I'm always finding out something new. I can't wait to let everyone else have a peek into the life of the *World's Most Prolific, Cinematic Killer.*

Michael Aloisi

MONSTER MANIA VIP

Horror conventions are a place where people who share a similar passion can get together to meet their idols, talk about their favorite films, dress up like the characters they love, see movies with like-minded people, buy souvenirs and party like... monsters. That's why when Kane invited me down to Maryland to attend Monster Mania 16, I didn't hesitate in saying yes.

Unfortunately, I have only been to a few conventions (mostly due to the fact there is not many in the Northeast), though if I could have my way, I'd go to one every weekend. If you have never been to a convention and you are a horror fan... stop reading this right now, do a search for one, book tickets and go. Getting to meet the killer's that haunted your childhood dreams and made you giggle with delight as adults is astounding. Sitting in on panel discussions about your favorite horror flick, with the actual stars, it's beyond words. Therefore, getting to attend as a guest of one of horror's greatest legends was unbelievable to say the least.

Due to major traffic, my wife, J.Anna and I arrived late to the hotel. We checked in around 10:30 and headed to meet Kane. As we walked down the hall, I

32

heard a deep booming voice telling a story that I instantly recognized. As we rounded the corner I saw Kane sitting in the hall surrounded by a dozen fans. I couldn't help but smile as I saw Kane taking time to sit and talk to fans, a lot of actors wouldn't do that, but he understands that it's the fans that keep the industry alive. He introduced me as the guy writing his book to his fans before we excused ourselves to go to the VIP opening night party.

Heading through the lobby I couldn't help but beam as I walked next to Kane. I watched people nudge their friends and point to us saying, *there's Kane f*cking Hodder!* I heard that more than once as we made our way to the party. As we strolled into the VIP reception, eyes from all over went to Kane. J.Anna and had to move quickly to keep up with him as he worked the room shaking hands and taking pictures. Finally we all settled on a spot and began to chat. As we talked about the weekend's events I looked around the room. To my right was Heather Langenkamp and five other actors from the *Nightmare on Elm Street* series. Two other guys who played Jason Voorhees were chatting to a *Friday the 13*th victim. Actors from them, *Night of the Living Dead, Boondock Saints, Terror Train, Puppet Master* and many other movies were all hanging, drinking and chatting only feet away from me. I was in heaven thinking things couldn't get better…and that's when Robert Englund walked over.

Kane introduced me to Freddy Kruger himself. As we chatted for a moment about Kane, I don't think I heard anything he said. All I could think was… I'm standing in-between Jason Voorhees and Freddy Kruger, hanging out, chatting. This was the equivalent of a religious fanatic standing between Jesus and God.

KANE IN ACTION

Though I had spent time with Kane before, I had yet to see him interact with fans. The last weekend we had spent together, we were a bit isolated. Only when we went out to dinner did I get to see him interact with fans. Even then, Kane was gracious enough to sign autographs *while* we were eating. In Maryland, we were far from isolated…horror fans were in every inch of the hotel.

The morning after the VIP party my wife and I went down to the convention around ten to meet up with Kane and watch him interact with his fans. He was set up in the autograph room with other celebrities. When we arrived, there was a line of fans waiting to meet "the legend". I stood off to the side wanting to observe Kane with his fans. I knew he had a pretty good sense of humor accompanied by a vicious sarcasm reflex, but I didn't realize just *how* funny Kane was.

One after one, fans came up, not being able to hide their smiles as they held out their hands to meet their favorite killer. Kane always met them with a smile or a sinister, joking glare followed by a firm handshake and a comment ranging from *hello* to a *what the hell do you want*. Sometimes he would just stare at the person

35

with their hand out, waiting for the right moment to quickly grab his machete (a real one mind you) and slam it against the table, making the fan jump and laugh. The sound was so sudden and loud all the people in the room jumped, every time.

Kane Signing a Fan's DVD

For two days I stayed with Kane, watching him taunt, tease, scare and make his fans happier than any of the other actors there. It didn't take long to realize that he was not scared to say or do anything to anyone. This became apparent when a hotel employee tried to use the phone that was mounted behind him on the wall. Instead of scooting out of the man's way, Kane ripped the phone off of the wall and handed it to the man who looked more than a bit shocked. Holding the phone in his hand, sheetrock dust covering his wrists, the employee nervously giggled as he looked at Kane's serious eyes and said, "No problem, uh, I'll, uh, have someone fix this later". When the man awkwardly hooked the phone on the wall and walked away, Kane just smiled a guilty grin and went back to signing autographs.

THE CHOKE

During our first visit Kane told me about how he hated pictures of people choking someone...they always looked fake. That's why he *really* choked people, to make it look good. I didn't think much of the comment at the time, even when I found numerous pictures of him online with his hands around a fan's neck. They looked realistic, but I just figured he was good at faking it...little did I know, Kane is crazy.

I'm a person that is, well, a wuss. I'm afraid of getting hurt, hurting others, breaking the law, getting in trouble and basically anything to do with pain or punishment. I even yell at my wife for not using her turn signal, when we are on a road with no one around for miles. It's why I enjoy horror so much; it's the complete opposite of me. Kane on the other hand, has no fear.

During that first day at the convention in Maryland, I watched Kane interact with the fans, signing autographs, shaking hands and taking pictures. When taking half of the pictures, maybe more, the fans *asked* to be choked. I saw the choke victim's faces turn red. At first I laughed thinking they were holding their breath for the picture, but then one by one, I started to notice the hand prints on their necks. Finally I said to Kane,

"You really freaking choke them, don't you?"
After laughing he went on to tell me about one fan that passed out and how he can usually feel things "pop" in people's neck. I think my jaw dropped at that comment.

Author, Brian J Orlowski Experiencing the Choke and Trying to Play it Cool

A few minutes after his explanation an expecting victim asked for a picture, Kane choked him. Afterwards, the man rubbed his neck and nervously laughed. Then, Kane told the guy to hold on and called me over.

"Put your hand on his neck." Kane said to me as the man's eyebrows rose with curious concern.

"What? Why?" I asked not really sure what he was going to do.

"Put your hand on his neck. You're writing my book, so you need to know what I do."

I'm not one for touching strangers, but I did as I was told and placed my hand on the front of the guy's neck, his Adams apple resting in the nook of my thumb and forefinger. Kane stood on the other side of the man and placed his gloved hands on the back of the guy's neck and on over my hand...then he squeezed. I stared at my hand around this guy's neck, not daring to look at the face going purple in front of me. Under my fingers I felt the sickest sensation I had ever experienced. It felt like grabbing a soft tube filled with slimy wires. I felt strands shift, move and crush together. Something hard popped and darted across the length of my finger and worst of all...there was a snapping, crunching feeling. Now, I can handle any horror movie in the world, hell, I'll clap and applaud it, but this...it made my stomach flip.

Finally, Kane let go and my hand slipped off the man's neck. My eyes searched the room as if to see if I got caught or not, or more so, to avoid having to look at the man who I had just choked. I could hear Kane laugh, knowing he had just shocked me. When I dared to look back to the man, he was smiling so big you would have thought he had won the lottery. He shook Kane's hand and thanked him over and over again before heading out the door. As I watched the man walk away, I saw Kane shaking another victim's hand out of the corner of my eye.

Later that day there was a *Friday the 13th* panel. Kane was the life of the panel, having the crowd laughing and cheering every few minutes. Then, at one point, when he was talking about how much he loves to play a killer he asked the crowd,

"How many of you mother f*ckers have I choked?" Instantly, well over half of the audience enthusiastically shot their hands up. Kane may be a bit crazy…but the fans freaking love it.

Kane on a Friday the 13th Panel

A KILLER WEDDING RECEPTION

After a long day of signing autographs and choking people, Kane, J.Anna and I went for a nice steak dinner and then back to the hotel bar for drinks. Being that the convention was going on, the bar was packed, and I'm talking, fight your way to walk ten feet packed. The fun part was that it wasn't your typical "bar crowd". Instead of button down shirts and designer jeans, the clientele were wearing ripped clothing, stained with fake blood. In addition to the celebrities, there were half a dozen Freddy's, Jason's, zombies, a "special" Frankenstein, Captain Jack Sparrow, random bloody people and one girl dressed as, well I can't even explain what she was other than the fact that she had three foot lifts on her shoes and she was wearing a lot of pink.

Kane and I walked through the bar and once again, I had to fight to stay with him. He zoomed around the room, shaking hands, getting patted on the back and taking pictures. We finally made our way to the actual bar and Kane and my wife ordered drinks. Of course, everyone wanted to buy their favorite killer a beer. As we stood waiting for the drinks I looked around the room. Personally, I hate bars, but one filled with bloody monsters wasn't so bad. As I checked out the different costumes and outfits I noticed that three

42

tables in the back were sectioned off. I thought that was kind of odd, considering Kane, Robert and the other celebs were at the bar. I decided to investigate. When I got close enough to read the signs I couldn't help but laugh, it read: *Reserved for Wedding Party*. I think for the umpteenth time that weekend, my jaw fell open. A wedding party? They were in for a monster of a surprise.

It's odd when people in cocktail dresses and suits stand out in a bar, but that night, when a group of well-dressed people came in, I instantly knew they were the wedding party. After fighting their way through the crowd they took up their seats and ordered *a lot* of drinks. Amazingly, there seemed to be no anger or disgust that there were unique and "bloody" people crowding their "special day". It might have been the alcohol, but after a mere twenty minutes or so…the wedding party was mingling with the horror fanatics!

Cute, young women were dancing, talking and laughing with Captain Jack and the "special" Frankenstein. Guys in ties were flirting with zombie and Goth chicks. And best of all, half of the wedding party was asking for pictures with Kane.

One particular woman in her late fifties, wearing a fancy black dress and white pearls, looking like a stuck up politician's wife, grabbed Kane by the arm and yelled,

43

"You played Jason? You scared the sh*t out of me in those movies!" She took a picture with him, and then proceeded to pull Kane around the bar to show him off to the other wedding guests. After a little while she finally left Kane's side and started to talk to a guy with a two foot Mohawk. I couldn't help but keep watching her as she touched it, then asked to try on his leather-studded jacket.

The entire time we sat there, I couldn't help but watch everyone and everything. I felt like a wild life photographer watching lions and gazelles happily playing together. I knew watching wedding guests and a horror convention partying together was a once and a life time event, but unfortunately, we were exhausted and we had to leave the wonderful circus to get some rest so we could choke some more people the next day.

THE KANE OF MY YOUTH

We all have certain movies that make an impact on our lives. My brother and I have about twenty movies that we watched over and over again during the late eighties to the early nineties. Having watched these movies a hundred times each with my brother, they have become a part of my childhood memories and hold a special place in my heart. They are the films that if I click by them on cable, I have to stop and watch them, even though I could recite every line. They hold such a special place in my childhood that when I found out Kane worked on a bunch of them…I was transported right back to my youth.

For about five years of my childhood, my brother and I wanted to be Ninjas. This was mostly due to the fact that we were obsessed with *American Ninja 2*. I don't remember if it was on HBO all the time or if we had it on tape, but the bottom line is we watched it on a daily basis, trying to perfect the ninja moves in the movie (my brother even took it as far as trying to make his own ninja stars out of tape and tinfoil). One day while talking to Kane, he mentioned *American Ninja 2*. I had to stop him and ask him to repeat what he said. He repeated the title… I had heard right. Kane worked on the movie that my brother and I recreated fights from for years. I tried to keep a

45

straight face, when really, I wanted to jump up and show him the deadly ninja moves I learned from the movie.

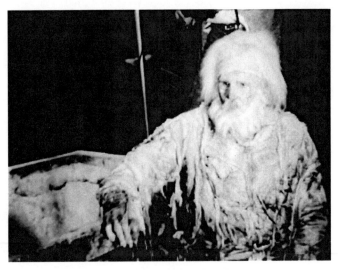

Kane Doubling as Gramps, *House II*

A few minutes later I found out that he was the stunt coordinator on the *House* movies and even had cameos in them. *House II: The Second Story* was another one of those movies we watched over and over again! Then, come to find out, Kane was in yet another movie we freaking loved, *Nothing But Trouble*. Though the movie was a huge flop, to us kids, it was hysterical, especially the two giant, oversized, creepy babies. Being a chubby little butterball at the age of twelve, my brother use to tease me that I looked like one of them…come to find out, Kane played one of the babies, Bobo, when Dan Aykroyd was playing another character. Every other minute Kane mentioned a movie I watched a thousand times as a kid... I was in heaven getting a sneak peek behind the movies of my youth.

Everyone knows Kane for being a horror legend, but his stunt and acting career spans much more than just monsters and killers. Kane's life is fascinating...and I can't wait to let all of you read about it in *Kill!*

SLEEPWALKING IN FLORIDA

When Kane suggested I join him in Florida for the opening of *Hatchet 2*...I was on the computer looking up flights before he could finish inviting me. The idea of getting to see the best new horror franchise with the star, AND go to all the press events for the film with him as well, had me packing my bags before I even got off the phone with him (and it was still two weeks away).

I flew down the night before the event; unfortunately, I could only get a late flight, which landed at midnight. Normally that wouldn't have been too bad, but our day was to start at 6:45 in the morning.... or so I thought. As I raced through the Raleigh North Carolina airport to catch my connections, I called Kane to check in with him. He was about to attend a midnight screening of the movie in Tampa and then have to drive over to Orlando. Kane said everything was all set, only instead of being picked up at 6:45...they changed the time to 6:00 a.m., which meant we had even less time to sleep.

The flight landed on time at midnight, though by the time I took the shuttle to baggage claim and found a taxi, I didn't get to the hotel until one in the morning. Exhausted, I checked in. The lone man behind the desk offered to have a bellboy drive me to my room, being that it was a resort it was massive and the walk to my room was rather long. Fighting to keep my eyes open, I agreed to the offer. The man disappeared into the back room and I was left alone in the cavernous lobby. I paced back and forth for a few minutes, trying to stay awake. Getting annoyed at having to wait I peeked outside, thinking maybe he was waiting for me; no one was there. I tried to look into the back room to ask the guy if he was coming, but he mysteriously disappeared. Finally, after ten minutes of waiting, I decided to walk to my room, how far could it be after all?

The fact that I was given a miniature map of the grounds should have been my first clue that I was not setting out on short jaunt. Holding my map I headed out the side doors, dragging my feet as I tried to figure out just where I was. There were paths that shot out in all different directions. Not being sure which way to hold the map, I wandered down path after path, deliriously drunk with lack of sleep. My mind clouded with images of the bed that lay at the end of this journey. As I stopped by a small pond to once again find my location, I heard a loud hissing noise behind me...it was the sprinklers turning on.

Not only was I exhausted, I was now wet and still lost. I circled around several pools, a bar, a gift shop, ponds, a gym and countless rooms all while trying to avoid the sprays, unsuccessfully. After twenty minutes (seriously), I started to debate sleeping under the bushes. I would have too if I hadn't see about a dozen little lizards scurry across my toes.

Then, like finding the Holy Grail, I ran right into building number 9, where my room was. Drying off my key I opened the door and entered the hallway, a tiny bit of energy pouring into me, enough to get me to my room. Reading the number I realized that my room was on the opposite side of the building, wanting to cry as my feet sloshed down hall after hall. When I found my door it was like winning the lottery. Ten minutes later I was in the bed, trying to figure out how to set the alarm. I was almost laughing I was so delirious. With the alarm set I forced my mind to do the math…. three hours, I had three hours to sleep before I had to get up and spend the day with Kane….

HATCHET 2 PRESS TOUR

After what felt like a long blink, I awoke and hurried out of my hotel room (extra early to navigate the long walk). Being before six in the morning, the lobby was still desolate and the sun was still down. I was a bit early, so I sat down on a bench outside and tried *not* to fall asleep. I kept telling myself that Kane had it worse; he had to do a midnight showing, went back to his hotel for a mere two hours and then had get back up to drive at four in the morning over to Orlando.

After a few head droops, a big black Escalade pulled up and out jumped our liaison for the day, Craig. The chauffer stayed in the car. Craig came over and we chatted for a few minutes. As we talked about *Hatche*t, Kane called and said he was a few minutes away; I took this time to run to the bathroom. When I came back outside I heard loud booming laughing; I instantly knew it was Kane. Once again…he had scared someone. Having parked in the side parking lot, no one had seen him come in. He used the opportunity to sneak up in the darkness and pounce on the poor chauffer who was reading the paper in the driver's seat. Though I didn't see it, I was told the scare almost added a stop at the hospital to our long list of appearances that day. Trying to keep my eyes

51

open I looked at Kane. I was in awe; how could a man with even less sleep than myself be up to scaring someone that early in the morning? Only Kane... only Kane.

Kane Doing a Radio Interview

The car ride was filled with mostly grunts as we were all trying to shake the sleep from our heads. As we arrived at the first radio station of the day, the sun was just coming up. Realizing it was finally morning seemed to help us wake up a bit. We were greeted at the door and escorted upstairs. As we started to walk down the hallway, two dozen cheerleaders dressed in full uniforms, pom poms and all, cut us off. Kane turned and looked at me with a look that made me burst out laughing. When they finally all passed by,

Kane said, "What the f*ck was that! That is so not fair! You can't parade a line of cheerleaders past me and not expect all of them to live." As we laughed shaking our heads we entered the waiting area to go on air, newly invigorated as if the cheerleaders were our morning caffeine shot.

A few minutes later Kane and I were in the studio with Crash and LT, local Orlando DJ's. They asked some good questions that Kane zinged back answers to. As Kane was on air, I stood off to the side recording it on my Flip camera. You can go on our website, www.KaneHodderKills.com to watch the video!

THE OLD DOOR GAG

After three radio interviews, it was a bit after nine and we finally had a small break. Though we were desperate for sleep, eating was our top priority. As Kane and I gorged on the hotel buffet breakfast, we finally had some time to catch up and chat about the book. Only problem was, our waiter was so odd that we kept watching him instead of talking, especially when he asked to take a picture with a family of five that just finished breakfast. He clearly didn't know them and yet he took five pictures with his arms wrapped around the family members... four of which were just with the kids.

After our interesting breakfast, Kane checked into the hotel and we drove to our rooms (still exhausted, I was thankful to not have to walk). Of course, being Kane it wasn't a simple two-minute drive. No, not at all, he decided to drive the entire way to our buildings going down *One-Way* roads...the WRONG WAY! The first one, I believe, or more so I hoped, was by accident. I think he got a kick out of seeing my fright and how I grabbed my seat belt for safety and purposely drove down the wrong way the rest of the drive. Thankfully it was only on the resort grounds and no one else was on the roads.

After a quick thirty-minute break in our rooms (that was more torture than a break, the bed was calling my name and I didn't have time to sleep), we were once again back in the SUV on our way to another interview. This time Kane was scheduled for a television interview on *Orlando 13 News*. When we entered we were greeted by the anchor that was going to interview Kane, the beautiful Allison Walker.

Allison Walker, The Poor Victim of Kane's Door Gag

We chatted casually as Allison led the way down a long hallway. When we reached a big glass door, Kane, always the gentleman grabbed the handle to open it for the lady. Of course, in true Kane style, he couldn't just open it. Oh no, he had to do his classic door slams into his face gag, by kicking the bottom at the same time as throwing his head back. Being Kane, he is a pro at making it look too real. This was evident by the look on Allison's face. The anchor's delicate features twisted into horror, fear, dread and finally shock as she realized Kane was joking. Standing behind Kane in just the right position I was able to see all of these reactions. The following is a translation of what I saw on Allison's face: *Holy sh*t! Oh, my God, is he ok? I just let an actor smash his face… this is bad. He is going to sue; I'm going to lose my job. Is he bleeding? Wait a second, is he…he's kidding? That f*cking, a**hole.* Of course I have no clue what she *really* thought, but in the course of two seconds I saw more horror, shock, and relief than I ever had on someone's face.

Allison ended up being the best interviewer of the day, having done extensive research on Kane and his films. Not only did that impress us, she was also wearing a number 13 necklace, Kane's lucky number, and come to find out, hers as well.

ED DONOVAN LADIES AND GENTLEMEN

By the afternoon Kane and I were getting pretty punchy. We were laughing at stupid things and dragging our feet on the way to the press junket at the AMC Theater where we were to screen Hatchet 2 that night, which was in Disney's Pleasure Island district. When we got there, we were led into a very lavish green room with leather couches and autographed posters all over the walls. It was impressive seeing how many celebrities did events at that theater, though it made me sad since I'm sure my local theater does not have a room like that.

As we settled in Craig, our PR liaison, led in reporter after reporter giving them about fifteen minutes each to interview Kane. Most of the same questions were asked to Kane over and over again. I was getting tired of them, but Kane, even on his one hour of sleep, didn't lose his enthusiasm for answering the questions.

After several interviews, an old man rushed into the room and instantly Kane and I perked up. *Ed Donovan had arrived.* Not even a minute after he entered the room, Kane and I were cracking up. This man had more energy and enthusiasm than most of

57

the interviewers half his age. After five minutes of laughing and finding out amazing things, like the fact that Ed had been interviewed on *Oprah*, had a book written after his life and was now even an actor, I had to turn on my video camera. You can watch the interview online at www.KaneHodderKills.com.

Kane Talking with Ed Donovan

KANE CARES

After a refreshing nap and an energizing meal at the pool bar, Kane and I were ready to tackle the showing of *Hatchet 2* that night. When we arrived at the theater we met some contest winners who won the chance to see the movie with Kane and to receive some other goodies. After being introduced to them I stepped back a bit and let Kane talk to the two lovely women. I was amazed at how big of fans they were. They rattled off movie after movie that Kane had done, pulled out obscure facts that even I didn't know and proudly rattled off how many times they had seen each film. Kane was more than happy to listen and respond to their questions.

Now this quote doesn't seem like it should fit in when talking about *The World's Most Prolific, Cinematic Killer*, but watching Kane warmed my heart. Kane wasn't just humoring a fan; he was genuinely engaged in the conversation, wanting to talk to these ladies. I have seen tons of celebrities in my life that could care less about their fans. I remember being told at ten years old to "get away" from a certain football icon, when I asked for an autograph. I also had another celebrity take my pen and keep it; another signed a book of mine and tossed it aside, literally dropping it on the ground. I could go on about other experiences, but that is not what this is about. This is about how Kane is not one of those stuck up, too good to talk to his fans, types. Kane genuinely LOVES his fans. He is not pretending to pay attention or to care, he actually does. And that is rare. It's a major part of why I'm so proud to work on his book, because I know when it comes out, Kane will be happy to talk to his fans about his life story.

Kane with Friend/Fan, Elvis and Family

After almost fifteen minutes of talking, Kane had to be pulled away from the fans to get into the theater on time. He was so enjoying the conversation that he didn't want to stop it. When we got into the theater, Kane introduced the film to the other enthusiastic audience members. He even went out of his way to point out the winners. Then, instead of being one of those stars who leave the theater to do other stuff while it plays, Kane went up and sat next to the two winners and gave them a story they will always be able to tell their friends… getting to watch *Hatchet 2*, with Victor Crowley himself.

Though I have known how great Kane can be with his fans, our Facebook page is really giving me even more insight on the matter. Kane has received dozens of great comments from fans about their experiences with him, thanking him for being so kind. There have even been numerous emails thanking him for going out of his way at events. Every one of them makes me smile, because it ensures me that I couldn't be working with a better guy.

DETACHED TESTICLES, CURB STOMPS
AND HATCHETS = GREEN GOLD

Sitting down in the theater to watch Hatchet 2 for the first time, I was angry with myself for not getting popcorn. A good slasher film is always better with something to munch on. Even without a buttery bag in my lap, I was in heaven listening to Kane announce the film. My favorite past time has always been going to the movies, especially a horror flick. Since my wife doesn't like horror movies, it means that I'm usually alone in the theater watching in my own world of delight. This time however, I was getting to see the best new franchise, with its star, who was also one of my idols as a kid…*unbelievable.*

As the lights went down, I was a bit taken off guard; there were no ads, previews or even the AMC intro; the movie just started. And for those of you who don't know, it starts off from the exact frame the first one ended. Meaning, there is no easing into the movie.

Now, I'm not going to go on giving you a play-by-play review of the movie. If you want to read a review, do a search online. What I am going to say though, is that the movie rocks! I'm not saying this just because I'm writing Kane's book, I'm saying this as a horror movie fan. For one thing, there are more crazy kills in this movie than pretty much any horror film in history (it's so hard for me to not write about them here, but I don't want to ruin any of them), and not the sick uncomfortable torture kills of some of those other horror movies. I'm talking about laugh out loud, ridiculous, gory, insanely awesome kills. They're fun deaths that make you slap the person next to you and choke on your popcorn (okay, maybe it was good that I didn't have any). Not only is the film filled with some of the best kills in history, it is also, really, really funny. And to top everything off, Kane has some great scenes out of the make up as Victor's father.

I was a fan of the first movie. It was fun and entertaining. The second one however, I love. It is definitely one of the best slasher movies in the past few years, if not the decade. Adam should change his last name from Green to Gold, for he certainly is the golden boy of horror, even if his next movie is a children's film. I just wish it got a longer run in the theater so more of you could have seen it.

The fact that most of you have not gotten to see it because of it being pulled from the theaters early is heart breaking. I'm not going to get into the whole MPAA fight here; it is what it is and we can all complain, but the bottom line is that if you want to see unrated and independent horror films in the theater, you need support them by going out and buying tickets. So when Hatchet 2 comes out on

DVD (which when I talked to Adam last week he said they were trying to push it for a quick release), go out and buy a copy, buy two, heck, buy your whole family copies!

And if you haven't seen Adam's *Frozen* yet, get off your asses and go buy a copy TODAY. I wouldn't call it horror like it is labeled, but it is a top-notch thriller that will keep you tense the entire time. AND, Kane was the stunt coordinator on the film and has a cameo in it!

ROCK AND SHOCK
SHOPPING

Unfortunately, Kane couldn't attend the Rock & Shock horror convention in Worcester, Massachusetts this year due to a previous engagement in Mexico. Being that I live in Mass, I took the opportunity to go to the convention as a fan and... to talk to a few of Kane's friends and co-workers.

J.Anna, my wife, and I drove out to the convention early on Saturday. I was eager to meet more of my horror favorites and to see what the vendors had to offer. We walked into the vendor floor first. Booth after booth J.Anna had to stop me from buying a dozen items I wanted. There were a few booths that I did have a hard time walking away from. I don't really like to "plug" items. That is not the purpose of this journal entry. At the convention I simply fell in love with three artists' work, artists that used Kane as a subject. I think they are so terrific that I'm doing everything I can to work with them and to let other fans know of their work.

The first artist was Joel Robinson. The second I saw the large print of Kane's Jason Voorhees under water, I stopped in my tracks and rushed over to the booth.

65

There were dozens of pictures of horror icons lining the booth; the work blew me away. We got to talking with Joel about how I'm writing Kane's book. After a few minutes I noticed a poster on the table, an amazing collage of all the Jason's. I instantly snapped it up to buy. He even had the "Twelve Jason's of Christmas Cards" for sale... a must have for any horror fan. His work was so impressive that we are hopefully going to commission him to paint something for the book.

Poster by Joel Robinson

The next thing that caught my eye was a prize for a raffle- a beautiful, yet creepy stained glass panel of the *Friday the 13th Part 4* poster. The piece was gorgeous, elegant, but yet, a piece of horror memorabilia. It was fantastic. It was the only item of the kind at the booth, but thankfully, there was a business card under it. I was so impressed by it that when I got home I contacted the artist. Seeing other horror posters he had created in glass, I knew we had to get him to make some exclusive items for our site. The last few days we have been working on coming up with some amazing stained glass that Kane's fans are going to love!

The other booth that had me drooling was the Horror Icon's booth. I met Neil, the owner, at Monster Mania a few months before, but I had not had a chance to see his work. Finally, I got to see some of his stuff. When I was younger, I used to collect horror figurines. I loved the things and still have them (though my wife makes me keep them in the closet). I thought the detail on them was great until I saw Neil's work. His company makes limited edition, large sculptures of horror icons, figures that are, to say the least, amazing! Best of all, on display, they had a huge sculpture of Victor Crowley from *Hatchet*. It had crazy detail and it even came with an autographed plaque from Kane.

Michael Aloisi

After seeing all of the stuff my wife wouldn't let me buy, it was time to go talk to some more of the monsters from my nightmares.

ROCK AND SHOCK
THE STARS

After drooling over numerous horror themed items we made our way into the autograph room. After awkwardly walking past the cast of the Human Centipede (I couldn't look them in the eyes), we rounded the corner and bumped into Jake Busey. He was busy with a fan so we walked past him and went in the room. No matter how many conventions I had been to, the excitement of being in a room with a dozen movie stars, doesn't stop me from getting excited. George Romero, Danny Trejo, Adrienne Barbeau, Dee Wallace, all the girls from the new Halloween, Pinhead, the *other* guy from *Bill and Ted's Excellent Adventure*, Bill Mosley, William Kat, Adam Green and others were all around me... I was in heaven.

Though I wanted to meet several stars while I was there, my main goal was to talk to Adam Green, Danielle Harris, Doug Bradley and William Kat. Kane had worked with all of them and I wanted to get some quotes and stories. We first waited in line for Adam Green. As we got closer to the front we noticed that he had a small hand written sign on his table saying *I don't charge for autographs, because I love you.*

Michael Aloisi

Watching Adam with his fans, I could see how much he was enjoying hearing from them, just like Kane. When we finally got to meet him, we chatted for a few minutes, but we didn't want to hold up his line so we moved on and decided to go to his talk later in the afternoon.

Me and Adam Green

Kane had told me a lot about Adam and I had seen several interviews with him. He sounded like a cool guy, but it wasn't until I heard him talk that I realized just how funny and interesting he is. He was such a good speaker that when he was done, my wife turned to me and said, "I could listen to him talk all day." Unfortunately with the crazy schedule we didn't get to spend much time talking with him, though he did say

70

he would write something for Kane's book. After hearing him talk, I'm sure whatever he writes will be funny, interesting and true.

Though I didn't admit it to her (due to the fact that I was a bit nervous and that my wife was standing next to me), I have had a crush on Danielle Harris for years. And unlike a lot of celebrities I've met, Danielle was even more beautiful in person. It was hard for me to not stumble over my words as we chatted about Kane. Thankfully she was very personable and had a really funny, crass side to her. With about two dozen swears thrown in she told me a story about Kane...

Me and Danielle Harris

Leading up to the release of *Hatchet 2*, Danielle and Kane did a bunch of conventions and events together. Their signing tables were always next to each other since they got along great, always teasing and joking. For several events in a row, Danielle kept smelling this horrible stench. After the second time she started to get self-conscious, concerned people would think it was *her* that smelled. Event after event the smell kept coming back. After thinking that the smell was forever going to follow her, Danielle's sister accompanied her to an event.

"It's Kane! I saw him spray something; he just put it in his bag!" yelled her sister. After a quick investigation, Danielle finally realized that Kane had been spraying this stuff called "Pump a Dump" behind her for weeks. Basically it's a spray that smells like...shit. Danielle was pissed, but in a good way, one where she swears revenge.

Personally I have experienced this stench myself. Before I left Orlando after the *Hatchet 2* press tour, Kane and I were sitting on his balcony talking about the book. I heard about this spray before, so I asked him about it. Giddily, Kane got up and ran into his room to get it for me to smell. Back outside he spritzed a few sprays in the air, of course, almost right over me. A light mist of crap stench landed on my shoulders right before my flight. The stuff smelled like cow manure to me, though I have heard a variety of different smells in the description of this product.

I love the fact that Kane still pulls off practical jokes, especially when he carries one on for so long. We all need a good laugh and a good scare every now and then and Kane is simply the man who delivers them.

The Infamous Pump-A-Dump Spray
Kane's Prank of Choice

ROCK AND SHOCK
THE STARS PART II

J.Anna and I stood in the middle of the autograph room at Rock & Shock assessing the lines, figuring out who to talk to next when one of the best bad asses in film walked by, Danny Trejo. I have been a fan of his for years, his cool bravado, steely cold look and menacing tattoos and muscles always made for one of the best bad guys in the movies. When I saw him, I could not believe his size. On film he looks like this monstrous hulk that could destroy anything, when in reality… he was so small that when I turned to my wife, I saw her mouth was wide open staring at him.

"Is that really Danny Trejo?" She finally asked when her mouth closed. I irked out a yes as we both stared at him walking away. I couldn't believe he hardly came up to my shoulders, granted I'm a big guy, but still. After getting over the shock, I was still in awe at seeing him. In fact, I even respected him all that much more for being able to pull of someone you would not want to mess with.

Getting over the excitement of seeing Trejo, we finally decided to make our way over to Doug

Bradley's table. For those of you who don't know (and if you don't, I will shed a tear for you), Doug played Pinhead in ALL of the Hellraiser movies. Looking at Doug you wouldn't expect that he was one of the creepiest horror icons in history. Tall, skinny and with a British accent, Doug seems the farthest thing from the evil, flesh tearing Cenobite he played. After introducing myself and telling him the title of Kane's book, Doug told me how Kane once, after boasting about how many kills Jason had, asked him how many "kills" Pinhead had. Doug merely replied with, *I wouldn't know, Pinhead does not keep track of his kills, he is not a nerd.*

Me and Doug Bradley

After getting to talk to my first Cenobite, we headed over to meet William Kat. Now, I have no clue why, but I got nervous talking to Kat. I stumbled over my words, bumbled through my explanations of who I was and even stuttered a bit, which is not normal for me. The odd part is I just met the man I was scared of in my youth, that my brother made me watch over and over again when I was a teen, and I was fine. Even now I can't figure out why I got nervous around Mr. Kat... maybe because he is *America's Greatest Hero?*

Regardless of how stupid I looked, I got out the main question I wanted to ask him. Kane was the stunt coordinator on the set of the 80's classic, *House*, which starred William Kat. Kane told me a story from the set that involved him and Kat. I don't want to spoil it by writing about it here, in case I put it in the book, but let's just say I didn't know if Kane was exaggerating or not, well... he wasn't.

With my face burning red with embarrassment, we sauntered off. Our duty was done; it was now time to enjoy the convention.

FEELING THE BURN

At first, when I sat down to write *Kill!* I thought I was going to write about Kane's burn right off the bat. I wanted to write the hardest part of the book first, get it out of the way, set the tone and then move onto the fun stuff like stories from movie sets and anecdotes with other actors. It didn't happen that way though. When I sat down, ready with my notes, research and transcripts to write about this traumatic incident, I just couldn't do it. I wasn't ready to put myself in the place. Instead, I decided to start writing Kane's story from the beginning.

Writing about Kane's youth, growing up on tropical islands and his first ventures with stunts has been a great warm up, but still, I don't think anything has prepared me to write about the burn. For those of you who don't know, writing can be a very emotional process. When I'm writing fiction, I do everything I can to get into my characters' minds and feel what they feel. There have been numerous times that I found myself crying while writing an emotional scene which is why I have been tiptoeing around writing about the incident. I just haven't wanted to put myself into Kane's shoes during the ordeal. It was hard enough just hearing about the horrors that he had to deal with. The day Kane and I talked about his burn was emotionally exhausting for both of us. Putting myself into that mindset and having to live it through words, for days on end, is going to be hard, especially since it's not just some simple story of getting burned and healing. Kane's ordeal lasted for over a year and a half, spending six months in the hospital and over a year in recovery. It is so hard writing this part of his life that I'm taking a break from the book to write this.

When I was in my teens I worked in a restaurant as a cook. I would get burns all the time, small penny or quarter size burns from pans, sauce splatter and oven grates. Though they were small and only first-degree burns, they still hurt like a mother and ruined my day for weeks. A small burn on my hand would sting any time something touched it. Putting my hand in my pocket to get something was excruciating. I would curse the pain, treat the wound like a baby and try to be more cautious in the kitchen. Those tiny burns that I still vividly remember today are not even a fraction of what Kane suffered. His burns were third-degree, not first, *and* worst of all, they were over fifty percent of his body. There is absolutely no way to express in words the pain that he endured and eventually overcame. I just hope I can come close to conveying the depth of his suffering.

KILL! UPDATE

As time is flying by I figured it was time for a quick update on several things. Below is what is currently going on:

The Book

I'm still deep into Kane's burn story. It's such an immense, long story that it has taken up several weeks of writing. It has been hard and painful, but I'm getting through it and I feel like I'm getting the story across the way it needs to be told. I believe it will be as emotional for readers as it was for me to write.

Hopefully I will be out of the burn stuff soon and get to move on to more enjoyable and entertaining stuff to write.

The Store

Within a week we will be launching the official store for *Kill!* We just had some great t-shirts and hats made up and we have amassed several other great, unique items for the store. You'll be able to get handmade replica Jason masks made by the great Jeff WickedBeard *and* autographed by Kane himself!

There will also be some amazing, one of a kind, exclusive, stained glass movie posters from two of Kane's movies, each of which will be handmade by Joe Olson. Along with several other items, those of you who have been inundating us with emails asking for autographed pictures, you'll finally be able to get them! You will even be able to get autographed *real* machetes! Keep checking our posts for more information on the launch.

Conventions

Currently, Kane is at a convention in Germany called the *Weekend of Horrors*. He'll be there through the weekend. Those of you over there, get out and see him, it's not often that your favorite killer gets to go overseas to meet his fans.

December 3, 4, 5, Kane will be at the Steel City Con toy convention in Pittsburgh, Pennsylvania along with Lou Ferrigno. If you are in the area, make sure you come out and see him. I'll also be there for a few days myself to hang out with Kane and to work on the book.

Movies

Kane has a whole slew of movies coming up. He just finished filming another movie with Adam Green, called *Chillerama* where he plays a Frankenstein character named Meshugannah. Joel Moore (from

Hatchet and *Avatar*) plays Adolph Hitler, and yes it is a comedy. Kane also just got cast as Little John in a new version of *Robin Hood* along with Tom Savini who will play the Sheriff of Nottingham. *Room and Board* will feature Kane along with a top-notch cast that includes Burt Reynolds, Robert Loggia, William Kat and numerous other film greats.

Next weekend, Kane will be filming a part in a movie called *Cut*, which also stars Tony Todd and Michael Berryman. They will be filming on location in West Virginia. I'm thrilled that I will be able to join Kane on this shoot to get to see him work in person for the first time. Sadly, I will only get to be on set for the last day of filming due to my schedule.

For those of you who don't know, Kane has a ghost hunting team called Hollywood Ghost Hunters. Whenever he can, Kane goes out and hunts for spirits. He'll actually be on an episode of *Ghost Adventures* on the Travel Channel soon (we'll post more on it when we get the date). I myself have always loved ghost stuff. When my brother and I were kids, we would try to contact spirits and record ghosts on our tape recorders, though we have never had the courage to do an actual ghost hunt. Well, the day after shooting in WV, Kane is trying to set up for the two of us to do a hunt at an abandoned insane asylum. Yes, you read that right, ABANDONED INSANE ASYLUM. I never try to hide the fact that I'm well, not too manly. I can sit through any horror movie, but you jump out at me in person and I'll scream like a little girl. While I'm obsessed with horror movies and ghosts, I usually enjoy that stuff from the comfort of my couch or a nice movie theater seat. Just the idea of going into an abandoned insane asylum, even in the daylight, makes my heart race. Doing it at night, alone, with just Kane (who is also a killer mind you), makes me... excited (which translates to scared to death. *Note to self, pack adult diapers*). I'm sure you'll have a lot of journal entries to read after that weekend!

DON'T SAY HIS NAME THREE TIMES

After a ten-hour drive, my wife, J.Anna, and I arrived in Wheeling, West Virginia to meet Kane for the weekend. After checking in at the hotel, we called him and waited in the hotel lobby. Though we were only sitting twenty feet from the elevator, when Kane got off of it, it took him several minutes to get to us as he was asked for a few autographs. Seemed the hotel staff had been waiting for him. When he finally got away, we said our hellos and sat down to catch up for a few minutes.

Kane was in WV filming a movie called *Cut* directed and written by Joe Hollow. For the past three days he had been filming scenes with Michael Berryman (of the *Hills Have Eyes 2* and *Weird Science* fame) and Tony Todd (the legendary Candyman himself). Kane said the filming was going well and that he had killed Berryman the night before, finishing Berryman's scenes. I was hoping to get to meet him, but he left earlier that day. Kane and Tony on the other hand still had to film a few more scenes together.

As we were chatting, the elevator doors opened up and Tony Todd came out. I tensed up a bit; I was really looking forward to meeting him. When I was a kid, *Candyman* scared the piss out of me. I remember the night after I saw the movie I stood in the bathroom with the lights off. Looking into the mirror, I said his name once, licked my lips, grabbed the sink edges and said it again. Just as I was about to say it a third time, I heard a creak in my house. After nearly fainting, I ran to my bedroom, got under the covers and hid under the covers swearing to never say his name three times. Not only do I love *Candyman*, I had been a fan of Tony's other work for years. *Platoon, The Rock, Hatchet 1, 2* and countless others are on his resume; the man is great talent. To top everything off, Tony was the last piece of my horror icon puzzle. I had met every horror legend, except for him… and now I was not only about to meet him, but spend the rest of the night in his company.

When you meet an actor for the first time you usually have your expectations of what they are going to be like: small, big, nice or mean. I was expecting Tony to be a big guy, but in fact, he was huge. I'm a big guy myself, 6'2", 270 pounds, but when Tony came into the room, I felt like a munchkin. His hand engulfed mine as we shook hello. Wearing a long trench coat and a fedora, he sat down and relaxed as we started to chat. He had this carefree presence about him when he sat back that reminded me of a mafia boss with a heart of gold or a legendary musician just after a great set. To put it another way, he oozed coolness.

Tony Todd and Myself on the Set of *Cut*

As we spoke with Tony we quickly found out that he grew up twenty minutes from where J.Anna and I live in Springfield, MA. He was from Hartford, CT. He used to drive up to my hometown of Agawam, MA to go to the local theme park, Riverside Park (now Six Flags New England). Having this in common instantly gave us a lot to talk about, which was nice. It eased the "uh oh, what if I have nothing to talk about with this guy" fear that comes with meeting a lot of celebrities. After a few minutes the director, Joe, came over and we were introduced to him. He was busy getting ready for the night's shoot, but he was more than friendly to J.Anna and I as he welcomed us to his set as if we were a part of his family. After that, a production assistant arrived to take us to dinner before heading to the movie set.

A KILLER MEAL

For dinner, we went to the local *Quaker Steak and Lube*, a franchise I had never been to before. Of course, being that it was a Saturday night, there was a long wait. When you have two celebrities with you though, that is not a problem. Tony had been there earlier in the day to get some wings for after the shoot, so he had already met some of the staff. When they saw him again, they scrambled to get a table ready. As we waited, one of the wait staff came up to Kane and asked him if it was okay to get an autograph...from Tony. Apparently Kane had been mistaken for his bodyguard. Kane, getting a kick out of this said *"Oh, of course! Whatever you want from him."*

As we were about to be seated, the timid, but overly nice PA (Production Assistant), Keith said he would wait in the car for us. Both Kane and Tony yelled at him to not be ridiculous and to come eat with us. Seeing this made me happy, for I have seen some stars treat PA's worse than slaves. Reluctantly, though excited at the same time, he decided to join us. We were quickly ushered through the gas station themed restaurant and sat under a *real* yellow Corvette, which was hanging upside down from the ceiling. We quickly calculated who would die if it fell and then proceeded to look at the menus.

When our drinks came I quickly noticed they all had bright colored swirly straws in them. Being the dork I am, I was excited to watch my soda flow up the twisty tube. Kane did not share this sentiment. As I looked up from my first sip I saw Kane pull out his straw, straighten it and stick it back in ice tea. The only problem was, it was now four times the length of a normal straw. Kane gave it one look, pulled it out and threw it over his shoulder.

"That straw is f*cking ridiculous. All I need is someone to snap a picture of me drinking out of that and put it online. Learned my lesson before... f*cking Macarena." As he went on to explain the Macarena story, I watched Tony looking at his straw. When Kane finished talking, Tony pulled out his own straw and tossed it on the table.

"Damn it, now you are making me self-conscious." Of course *I* kept using my fun straw though.

More than once during dinner I had to stop in mid chew and look at the two men in front of me. I couldn't believe it; I was eating a meal with Tony Todd and Kane Hodder. I did my best to squish my smiles, but it was hard. Here I was, breaking bread with two of my childhood nightmare idols. And not only that, we were about to go and watch them film a movie. Life was good.

The rest of the dinner was great. The conversation flowed, we learned more about Tony and realized that Keith the PA and J.Anna and I had a mutual friend in common. Just as we were finishing up, the manager came over and asked Tony to sign an autograph for the restaurant. Kane smiled, keeping up the illusion that he was the bodyguard, until Tony told the manager the truth. Instantly the man ran and got another piece of paper for Kane to sign. On the way out they were stopped once again to take pictures with the staff, which they more than happy to do, even if they were already late to the set. The manager, giddy to have his own picture taken, ran in the back and got a *real* eight-inch chef's knife for Kane to use in the pictures. Of course, Kane held this real, very sharp knife tight to a few lucky picture-takers necks. Just as we were about to walk away, Tony noticed a large backdrop of a bucket of hot wings that you could stand behind and put your faces into to cut out holes to make it look like you are part of the pictures.

"Kane, we've got to do it!" Tony said with a touch of glee in his voice.

"No f*cking way, we take that and it will be all over the Internet tomorrow. *Jason and Candyman have fun with chicken.*" Though Kane was reluctant, Tony wouldn't take no for an answer. Eventually Kane caved in and walked around the board to put his face on a spicy buffalo wing. Three cameras snapped off, sadly not one of them mine as it was in the car. As Kane walked back around to the front he was grumbling, but I could see that he really enjoyed it.

Kane will probably kick my ass for this, but here is the picture that the manager emailed me.

Tony and Kane Having Buckets of Fun!

TATTOOS, SCARS AND WINGS

As we arrived at the West Virginia State Penitentiary, I was giddy. I had seen this gothic prison on *Ghosthunters*, *Ghost Adventures* and several other "Haunted Places" shows. Pulling in, I was in awe. The architecture itself was worth the visit. Though at the same time, the 1800's design makes it look…creepy to say the least, especially under a full moon, which it was that night.

Getting out of the car inside of the gates, I was more than surprised when I heard *Baby Got Back*, pumping from inside one of the buildings.

"Ah sh*t, they are having that stupid wedding." Kane said before I could even ask what the hell was going on. *A wedding?* Now I was confused. Turns out, they rent out the newer addition of the prison for functions… including weddings. We entered the building and went to the craft services area, about ten yards from the thumping music. Over some cheesy 80's song that the wedding party was singing along to, Kane introduced J.Anna and I to several of the crew members. From there, we headed back to *wardrobe* so Kane and Tony could get in their costumes.

Once they were dressed, we joined the two in *make-up* as they got made up for shooting. Kane's outfit for this particular scene was a white tank top, which left his shoulders and chest, the worst of his scars from his burn, exposed. I had seen some of his scars, but I hadn't seen his chest close up before. Having written about the burn for the past few months, it was hard to see the scars, for I know the pain that caused them. Amazingly, what I didn't know, was that he had a massive tattoo of fire, on his left shoulder, where the worst of his scars are. There was something poetic and beautiful about the tattoo. It is such a great statement, putting a picture of fire over burned skin.

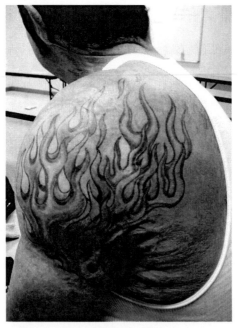

One of Kane's Tattoos

92

Talking about the flames, I learned that Kane actually had more tattoos that I didn't know about. Of course I knew about the *Kill!* tattoo on the inside of his lip, that is where we got the book's name after all, but I had no clue that he had a tat on each temple and one on his ankle. The ones on the temples are Chinese symbols and the one on his ankle is a chalk outline of a body, which I loved. The fact that I didn't know about his tattoos made me realize that even though we have spent hours talking about his life that I still had a lot to learn about Kane.

While we were talking about tattoos, Angie Savage, a well-known adult film star who was breaking into mainstream acting on *Cut,* joined our conversation. She was wearing a tank top herself and no bra at the time. She told us that she had angel wings on her back, turning around she showed us the tops of her shoulders, before saying *oh what do I care* and pulling her shirt off to show us her massive tattoo. The wings covered her entire back. We were all impressed to say the least.

With Tony's eye patch in place and Kane's fake stubble applied we were ready to head to set. As we opened the doors to head outside, I was more than a bit creeped out as a thick blanket of fog had settled in. The full moon made it glow with perfect eeriness of a horror movie. It was perfect, considering we were now about to enter the old, decrepit part of the jail... that was also haunted.

JAIL CELLS, TOILETS AND TEARS

To get to the filming location in the massive West Virginia State Penitentiary, we had to drive around the complex and enter a back gate into the giant old prison yard. It had to be the size of five football fields, but it was so dark and foggy you could barely see the outlines of the high stonewalls that use to keep the prisoners in. We parked and followed the few work lights towards the entrance. The second we walked in, the mood changed from creepy, to terrifying. The feeling could be attributed to the fact that there was a dead body on the ground, blood on the walls and a strobe light flashing. Come to find out, during Halloween they turn one of the floors in the prison into a haunted house. We walked right into part of it, which they just happened to not have cleaned up after yet. Thankfully, we were shooting a few floors up.

When we reached the landing at the top of the stairs, we walked past five people on their hands and knees trying to glue together a smashed toilet. "All the king's men couldn't put humpty dumpty together again." Someone joked as Kane checked the work. They were putting it back together for a stunt Kane was going to shoot that night. In the scene Tony and

94

Kane get into a fight in a jail cell. Tony gets the upper hand and slams Kane's head into the toilet, smashing it, hence why they were gluing a toilet together. The theory was that if they used a weak glue, when Kane smashed his head against it, it would fall apart. As Kane looked at the toilet I could tell he didn't seem too happy with how it looked. He made some jokes about it, but the prop guys reassured him several times that it would work and look good. With a shrug, Kane was ushered down the hall to see the set up for the first shot.

As we turned a corner, I was in awe. I had never really been inside a real prison before, let alone a closed down, decrepit, haunted one. Seeing the long row of cells, four tiers high, I felt like I was in a movie, which was odd considering I was on a movie set. The only light was coming from the productions lights that were set up for the scene. The bright spotty lights left massive dark spots and flickering shadows throughout the cellblock, adding to the mood. As Kane went over the scene with the crew, J.Anna and I looked around the cells… they were tiny. Inside one of the cells I felt like I was in a closet. It was so small, and yet two to three people use to be crammed into them.

Using the flashlight I brought along I surveyed the walls. Every inch of paint was peeling off. Beds were rusted and rotting off the walls, sinks were turning brown and the lights were filled with nests of bugs.

The prison had only been closed for fifteen years, yet it looked like it had been abandoned for a hundred. Stepping out of a cell I looked at all of the equipment, the dolly tracks, lights, boom operator and bounce boards hanging up and felt a pang of longing. I have two degrees in filmmaking and spent years in the industry before I left it to write full time. Being back on a set made me miss those old days. Pushing the memories out of my head, I moved closer to where they were about to shoot and watched Kane work.

Kane and Tony Preparing for a Scene, *Cut*

Together, Kane and Tony had created an entire back-story for their two characters. The first scene they were to film that night was a shot of the two of them in cells next to each other. Kane was going to do a monologue that he had written himself. The two kept whispering and chatting to each other as they planned out how they wanted the scene to go. The crew let the two do their own thing, only interjecting here and there to answer questions on the shots. When they were ready, the two stripped off their jackets (it was probably forty degrees in the prison) and got ready to shoot. Tony listened to some music on his headphones, singing along while Kane yelled a few times and got into character... two very different techniques, but you could tell it got both of them in the places they needed to be.

When the camera started to role, Kane started a monologue about being burned (they had worked his burns into the story). I don't want to spoil anything about the scene, but let's just say Kane gave a performance that literally had the director, my wife and three other crewmembers crying when he was done... seriously. After years of watching Kane on the big screen, it was amazing to be only a few feet away from him as he filmed a scene. Especially when it was one where he wasn't wearing make-up and he was giving such an emotional performance.

CEMENT HEAD

After a couple of hours of filming scenes in the cell, it was time to shoot the toilet-breaking stunt. Everyone cleared out of the way to let the FX crew bring the toilet in as they said it could fall apart at any second. With the toilet in place they put several pieces of cardboard next to it to give it support.

"No one enter the cell, the toilet is barely holding together, the slightest vibration could make it fall apart and we only have one chance to shoot this." Someone yelled from just outside the cell. Kane and Tony quickly got into their places, carefully. J.Anna and I got as close as we could to the cell, but it was so small that we could not see inside and the video monitor was already crowded, so we could only listen to the action.

The sound and camera rolled, the director yelled action and suddenly we could hear Tony and Kane grunting like mad men. There was a loud roar from Tony followed by a thunderous bang. I expected to hear clinking porcelain next, but instead there was dead silence for a breathtaking three seconds before Kane screamed a roar of anger. I looked to the crowd behind the monitor, two crew members had their hands over their mouths while the two director's jaws were hanging down in shock and panic... the camera still rolled.

"You can f*cking call cut!" Kane screamed from inside of the cell. One director sat, not moving while the other one got up and quietly said cut. The crewmembers all exchanged glances, wondering what was going on. The silence was then smashed by a loud thud as (I assume) Kane punched the wall. It followed by a stream of swears out of Kane's mouth. Eventually Kane emerged from the cell shaking his head, looking pissed as the characters he usually played. Though I was concerned for Kane, I couldn't help but chuckle as I watched one of the directors get up and quickly leave the set. Looking back to Kane I watched as Tony followed him and asked if he was all right or needed medical attention.

Imagine Trying to Break This Toilet with Your Head

"I'm alright, just f*cking rang my bell. The damn thing didn't budge! Going to fall apart my ass." I wanted to try and talk to him, but I didn't think it was my place to do so on the set; I was supposed to be watching after all. As I watched Kane pace back and forth, I could see the anger in his face. Behind his eyes the rage he was holding in burned bright. He let a few swears and choice comments slip out, but he didn't blow up. I could tell he was holding in his real anger at the situation, fighting it back. How couldn't he be pissed? He was told the thing was going to fall over if he sneezed, so he backed up and slammed his head as hard as he could on the lid… and the damn thing didn't even tremble. Honestly, I'd be surprised if he didn't suffer a concussion from the impact, an impact that *should not* have happened.

After listening to a few more swears, J.Anna and I suddenly found ourselves being escorted off of the set. We were asked to stay in the holding area and I begrudgingly obeyed. It was killing me not to see what was going on, but I understood the fact that they wanted a writer off of the set for such a mishap, so I did my best to stay put. Outside of the door I could hear arguing and screaming, not from Kane, but from crew members yelling at crew members.

"You almost sent Kane Hodder to the f*cking hospital! We are lucky he is alright, Jesus, he could sue, shut down this whole production…." The conversations and accusations went on and on.

Twenty minutes later, after my own pacing and even

laying down on an old rickety cell bed, I decided to go back out there to see if everything was all right. When I made it back to the set, I found Kane was fine and in good spirits, even if he did have a rapidly bruising, golf ball sized lump forming on his forehead. Come to find out, when he settled down, instead of storming off like a diva, he slammed his head into the toilet several more times until it broke. I think everyone was impressed by the fact that he would do it again, especially since he had to now hit a giant wound over and over again. I was impressed that Kane put aside his pain and anger...and got the shot done.

We later found out that the props builders changed the glue that Kane specifically told them to use. They said it wasn't holding because of the cold, so they switched to a much stronger, permanent glue...which is why it didn't break apart like planned. Even though Kane found out that the glue was switched on him without being told, resulting in him getting injured, he didn't get angry again. He understood that it was a low budget film with crew members that were just starting out in the industry, so instead of chewing them out, he gave them advice for future films.

Even though Kane was in pain and the incident was frustrating, in the end it got a good laugh. Everyone joked about it and Kane proudly showed off the lump, I got a story to tell, and Kane's nickname of Cement Head was confirmed.

WHAT NOT TO DO ON A FILM SET

On a film set there are certain rules that should be followed. Years of schooling and running my own company drilled these rules into my head. I never want to offend anyone or cause trouble, so I always make sure to abide by these unwritten guidelines. My wife on the other hand had never been on a film set. On the ride down to West Virginia I went over a long list of things she should and should not do when on the set.

The first rule, the obvious one, is to not get in the way. Time is money on a film set. If you hold up production by getting in the way, people are not going to like you. The next rule is to watch your step. With lights, cameras and tracks all over the floor, film sets are a death trap. Lastly and the most important, when they start to film, do not make a sound, not even a sniffle. The smallest of sounds can take an actor out of a scene or worse, be picked up by the microphone, ruining the take. Having sat through countless movies with my wife, I know how she can talk out loud at the screen without even realizing it. This idea scared me, so I drilled the "silence" rule into her head. Surprisingly, on set she was perfect. She didn't make a peep or get in anyone's way. She was great...

almost.

While Tony was doing some shots, Kane had a small break. Tony really wanted to get some t-shirts from the gift shop at the prison museum, but it was closing. Kane volunteered to go get the shirts, so we decided to drive Kane around to the front. We went down stairs, out into the foggy, pitch black courtyard and got into the car. It was right after the toilet incident so we started to laugh about the lump on Kane's head... the laughter didn't last long though as the back of the car suddenly sunk down with a loud scraping noise. We were stuck...

In a panic I jumped out of the car, switched on my flashlight and gasped. For some unknown reason, there was an open manhole and my wife had backed right into it. The rear driver's side tire was completely in the hole. Trying to drive in either direction would do nothing but destroy the tire; we were not getting out without a lot of help. Kane and J.Anna got out of the car to see what I was laughing at and joined my shocked reaction.

"So much for keeping a low profile" I joked trying to keep my wife from freaking out that her car could be damaged. Thankfully, she laughed. After a few minutes we decided there was nothing we could do at the moment.

"Guess we can walk to the store?" I said, not really sure if it was close enough to us or not. The three of us then headed through the fog covered field with only one flashlight amongst us. I was a bit worried that I'd turn and one-by-one they would disappear, having fallen into a manhole. Sweeping my flashlight back and forth to prevent this I tried to stay warm as the temperature had dropped. Oddly, the walk ended up only taking less than a few minutes, meaning, it would have been quicker to walk than it would have been to drive. We got stuck for no reason.

My Wife's Amazing Driving Skills

When we got back with the shirts, J.Anna and I sheepishly entered the set, not wanting to say a word about what happened. It might have already been one in the morning, but we could figure out how to get the car out *later*. Just as Kane started working on the next shot, one of the crewmembers came up and whispered in my ear.

"Is the white Honda yours?" Embarrassed, I said yes.

"We are going to try and get it out, but we don't want to touch it without you being there." Horrified, I followed him to the car, J.Anna trailing behind me. As we got outside I was surprised to see that they set up work lights to light up the car; it made me feel even worse as the lights felt like they were putting our mistake on display. Out of nowhere a half dozen crewmembers came out of the fog, one wheeling a two-ton jack. A quick discussion about how best to get the car out went around. In the end, the solution was to put the jack under the car, get it as high as possible and then have all six guys lift the car while J.Anna tried to drive. Amazingly, it worked on the first try. Miraculously, besides a small dent in the bumper, the car worked. If it hadn't been for the oddly thick manhole cover, the axel on the car would have snapped. Look carefully at the picture and you'll see the bumper is actually resting on the cover.

At worst, I thought that J.Anna might make noise during a shot, or possibly trip on a wire… instead, she shut down production while half of the crew helped get our car out! As much as I want to tease her about messing up shooting, it really wasn't her fault and other than that incident, she was an angel on set.

A PRANK IN THE ASS

Ever since the first time Kane jumped out and barked at me like a dog, scaring a few years off my life, I have learned that he loves pranks. On the set of *Cut*, Kane's pranks were in full swing.

The first prank I witnessed Kane do that weekend (five times, that I saw), was putting a large plastic box up against the bathroom door after someone went in. Kane is an equal opportunity prankster, so he did this to both men and woman that went into the rest room. When they opened the door to leave, the big box would slide down and slam onto the floor, causing them to jump. Seeing the reactions was interesting. Two people yelped and laughed a bit, yet another two thought they did something wrong and quickly picked it up. The last one, it didn't faze at all. He simply stepped over it as if he expected the loud crashing noise... maybe Kane already did it to him that night.

Around three, when the crew took a lunch break, Kane pulled a prank that made me nervous to say the least. Kane, J.Anna and I were eating some sandwiches when this young, *McLovin* (from *Superbad*) look alike, production assistant sat down with us. He had a big plate of pasta. After he set down his plate, he went to get a drink. Kane took this opportunity to strike. He tore off a piece of tinfoil from his sandwich wrapper, rolled it into a ball and stuck it in the kid's macaroni. Using his fingers he moved the pasta around to make sure it was covered up good so the kid wouldn't see it.

I can be a bit paranoid about things... I'm a borderline worrywart who always tries to avoid accidents and mishaps. Seeing the tinfoil go into this kid's food, the first thing I thought was... *Dear God, the kid is going to choke on it!* Keeping my eyes glued on the kid's pasta I went over the Heimlich maneuver in my head, making sure I could spring into action if necessary. Chatting with the kid, I started to sweat a bit as I was anticipating a tragedy. I started to think about how if the kid died Kane would go to jail for manslaughter and that would really mess up the book tour! Since I was staring at the kid, I couldn't help but notice how he was eating a bite of the deathly pasta, but then he would put down his fork and take a bite of a banana, something I thought was odd to say the least. *Macaroni and cheese with bananas?* In a way, I thought he was doing it to prolong my torture of waiting for the deathly bite.

Just as I was about to not be able to take it anymore, the kid's fork moved over the noodles to reveal the shiny ball of death. He discovered it himself and removed it, probably thinking the chef must have dropped it in by accident. I let out a sigh of relief so loud several people looked at me like I was having an asthma attack. Glad that the incident was over, I finally blinked and moved my eyes away from the plate… only to see Kane was doing it again to a guy sitting a few seats over from him. The worry knot in my chest tightened up again…Kane might be a *prank in my ass*, but it sure did make things interesting.

A BIG CHANGE

After filming all night at the West Virginia State Penitentiary, we all slept in late the next morning. Around one in the afternoon, Kane and I met up in the hotel lobby to work on the book. We asked the front desk if we could use one of the conference rooms so we would have a quiet area to work, but the guy gave us a hard time, saying we had to pay. Luckily, the head housekeeper walked by and saw Kane talking to the manager. After hearing about the situation, she declared that Kane could use the facilities however he wanted. Two minutes later we had a conference room, for the entire day to use, for free. The only catch was Kane had to sign some autographs. After a quick radio call, twelve maids were suddenly circling Kane and giggling. Graciously, he took a picture with each maid and then a final group picture. He didn't stop there though; Kane ran up to his room and got pictures of himself as Jason, came back down and signed one for each lady. The maids stood in line, giggling and taking pictures as they waited for Kane to sign a picture for them.

When we were finally alone we began the work. One by one Kane went down his list of film credits. Though I have poured over his IMDB list a thousand times, I was impressed to hear the extremely long list of films I *still* didn't know about, that IMDB didn't list. While he was talking, I found several clips of his work online: a great Taco Bell commercial he did with Jack Palance, a music video and a few other things. You can see both on our video page by visiting Kane's YouTube page.

Getting down to business, we started to talk about the release of the book and the work that goes with it. Our main concern was the release date. Originally it was set for Friday the 13th of May, 2011. It was a great date, being that it is the anniversary of the release of *Friday the 13th Part 7*, which was Kane's first appearance as Jason. The date was great, but, like always, life gets in the way. Kane has several movies coming up that will be filming in the spring. One of which might film in early May, meaning Kane would not be able to do press for the book release. Being that *Kill* is his life story, he wants nothing more than to be at every event he can to meet his fans.

We batted around several dates for a new release, but none of them felt right. Then we came up with October 1st. It was perfect. Halloween season would be starting... when is there a better time to pick up a book about one of the world's favorite killers? While we were saddened to push back the release, we both agree that this new date will be much better in the long run for all of us.

THE NIGHT BEFORE BLOODY CHRISTMAS

'Twas the night before Christmas,
When all through the house,
A creature was stirring and it wasn't a mouse;

Body parts hung by the chimney with care,
In hopes that Kane Hodder, soon would be there;

The children were tied all tight in their beds,
While visions of Jason Voorhees
Danced in their heads;

My wife in her nighty, and I finishing my nightcap,
Had just settled down for a long winter's nap,

When out on the lawn there arose such a clatter,
I sprang from the bed only to slip on brain matter.

Hitting my head, I saw a bright flash,
Ignoring the pain, I threw up the sash.

The moon was so bright it lit up the snow
Worried about werewolves,
I scanned the objects below.

When what to my fearful eyes should appear,
But a smashed up sleigh and eight dead reindeer.

Blinking my eyes,
I thought things couldn't get much odder,
For I knew in that moment,
It must be the legendary... Kane Hodder.

Ki, Ki, Ki... Ma, Ma, Ma,
Suddenly rang in my head,
Oh how I wished
I could just go back to bed;

"Now, Jason! Now, Victor! Now, Ed and BTK!
To Camp Crystal Lake! Then the bayou...
We'll slash away! Slash away! Slash away all!"

With the wink of an eye
I watched the killer break down my door,
Turning around to flee,
I found that my wife had left me... damn whore.

Down the stairs I ran,
Hoping not to find that large, hulking man.

Kane was not in sight as I looked all around,
But I did find my wife... all tightly bound.

From the doorway he came, all covered in blood,
With each step he took, came a bone chilling thud;

112

A sack of decapitated heads he had flung on his back,
He looked like a killer just finishing an attack.

His eyes -- how they glared!
Move... I would never have dared!

The goatee on his chin was as black as his heart;
I wondered, why did all of this have to start.

Menace encircled his head like a wreath;
He had a broad face and tight chest,
That was hard as his teeth.

His arms hardened, when he flexed with rage.
He was a jolly old killer,
Who should be locked in a cage.

I laughed when I saw my life flash before my eye;
As I knew one of us... was about to die.

Soon with one look, I had everything to dread;
He spoke not a word, but went straight for my head.

With a smile, he snapped my neck with a jerk.
He removed my head quickly...
I guess that was a perk.

Dropping my head, he gave it a kick.
Man, this guy was such a sick, dick.
My head rolled out the door,
And I was alive... no more.

113

Michael Aloisi

The last thing I heard, as I died that night,
Was Kane Hodder, wishing you all… a good fright.

"Merry Christmas to all, and to all… sleep tight."

**Even with Santa Smiling,
Kane Was Still on the Naughty List**

UNTOLD STORIES AND SEMEN

Kane and I haven't been able to get together over the past month, but we have exchanged countless phone calls going over information for the book. This extended period of time has given me time to work exclusively on the manuscript while Kane has been prepping for a few new movies as well as promoting the DVD release of *Hatchet II*. Which by the way is now out... and you all bought it already, right? You *better*, trust me, I have seen Kane pissed... you do not want that.

The downside to not spending much time with Kane is that I haven't had journal entries to write. Having realized so much time has slipped away since the last one, I decided to put together a bit of an update about the status of the book.

The book is about three-quarters of the way done. The past few weeks I have been working on the *Friday the 13th* stuff. I'm not sure why I waited so long to write these parts, but it might have to do with the fact that I'm a rabid fan of the series and wanted to savor spending the time writing about it, especially since I'm getting to tell stories that NO ONE has ever heard before. Behind the scenes stuff and things that happened with Kane that he has never talked about will be in the book. I gobbled up *Crystal Lake Memories* (the complete history of the series) by Peter M. Bracke with glee. It is the best book on the series and a must read for every diehard fan. Kane is in the book a lot, but there is still a lot of his feelings, emotions, thoughts and events that happened to him that have never been told. Getting to be one of the first people to ever hear these stories and to be able to tell them to his fans... it's a dream come true.

Kane has so many other great stories that will be in the book as well. Everything from mishaps with other celebrities, to how one really, really dedicated fan once mailed him a vile of semen. I swear, I cannot stop laughing every time I think about that story. It is insane! Over all, the book is coming together amazingly well. Kane's fans and even people who have never heard of him are sure to love this book.

Lastly, Kane and I will be heading to Florida in a few weeks to shoot the book cover along with some promotional pictures. Jesse Adair, the amazing horror photographer will be shooting the photos.

THE PAIN OF LETTING GO

For almost ten years I was a super-hero…really. For those of you who don't know my story, I worked for a division of Marvel Comics. I dressed up as Spider-Man and other super heroes doing live appearances all over the world. I did everything from store openings to touring the Pentagon and closing the New York Stock Exchange. It was an amazing and fun job that will be documented in *My Life in Spandex* which will come out in summer of 2012. During those years I was on TV countless times, in newspapers and all sorts of other media events. As I got older, I wanted to settle down and get married, so I slowly retired.

Even though there were other people playing the character besides me, I still felt like I was *the* Spider-Man as I did most of the major events. When I retired it was incredibly hard for me to let go. This was *my* thing. The thought of someone else doing my appearances killed me. At times I would get depressed when I found out that someone was doing an appearance that I would have normally done. Leaving that spotlight was hard to say the least.

Currently, I have been writing how Kane was screwed out of playing Jason in *Freddy vs. Jason*. After almost sixteen years of being the *only* person to play the

117

character in major films, Kane lost the role. I know how hard it was to let go of Spider-Man and I did it voluntarily. I can't fathom how hard it had to be for Kane. He never wanted to let go of the character and the loss was on a worldwide scale.

Writing this section in the book has brought up all of those memories and feelings of loss that I had and still have from time to time. Every year when certain events come up that I used to appear at year after year, I get sad knowing someone else is wearing that suit, entertaining the people I had become friends with over the years. Having to live through these emotions on a much larger scale has been gut wrenching. The worst part is the drama behind the situation and how it was all handled. It makes me sick.

Being a huge fan of the series, I have read all of the rumors and stories behind why he wasn't cast. Besides talking about how much it pissed him off, Kane has never really gotten in-depth about how much it affected his life... until now. Getting to talk to Kane and hear his truly deep emotions and feelings... it's moving and I think you guys will agree.

CODY BLUE SNIDER

Recently I got to talk to a friend of Kane's while doing the research for his biography. His story was so interesting; I had to tell it here. His name is Cody Blue Snider and he is the son of legendary rock legend, Dee Snider. This is his story about how he met Kane:

Cody was going to film school at The School of Visual Arts, which just happens to be where I went to college, when he got to read the script for Adam Green's *Frozen*. He loved it so much he told Adam, who he met through his father, that he would leave film school to work on the film in any capacity (he also said some other things, but we'll keep this clean). Sometime later, Adam gave him a call and said for him to fly out to Utah to where they were going to film.

With his father being a big horror fan, he had heard of Kane Hodder before, but he had never met him and didn't know what he looked like. When he got picked up in Utah for the first time he hopped in the backseat of a car next to some massive man with his arms crossed. It only took him a minute to notice the scars on the man's arm and that the big dude was not smiling or looking friendly at all. "I'm Cody," He said putting a hand out to this big man, trying to break the ice. The man looked at it, kept his arms crossed and spoke. "Did you fart?" Cody nervously said no and asked why, curious why this man was accusing him of something before he even introduced himself. The tough man looked Cody in the eyes and answered, "Because I smell cum." Of course... the big tough looking man was Kane.

It still wouldn't be for a few days until Cody and Kane would become friends. During one particularly frustrating day of filming everyone was in a cranky mood as they took a meal break. Being ever so energetic, he tried to be the jester of the group and make people laugh. Cody followed Adam around, telling Adam to punch him in the face, that it would make him feel better. Adam brushed it off, but Cody kept it up, begging and pleading with the director to take out his frustrations on his face. Fed up, Adam blurted out for Cody to have Kane punch him. Kane was behind them in line, Cody turned to him and said, "Hey Kane..." Without even being able to finish the sentence, Kane punched Cody right in the face... down to the ground he went.

The room went silent shocked that Cody's head didn't go flying off. Shaking it off, he got up and faced Kane, rubbing his jaw. It was the first time he saw Kane smiling big. "Okay, I hit you, now you hit me." Kane said, welcoming retribution. The room filled with murmurs as no one thought he would do it. Even though he was facing one of the world's greatest killers, Cody used the martial arts training he had as a kid, jumped in the air and landed a super man like punch to Kane's face. While Kane hardly budged, the big man was impressed and offered his hand to Cody. "Alright... Alright." He said while shaking Cody's hand, as if he was complimenting him.

The next day Kane went up to Cody and told him that no one had ever taken him up on that offer and actually punched him. From that moment on, the two became fast friends and hung out on the set, often exchanging jokes and insults.

Some people get to know each other over a nice meal, perhaps working together for a while... or if you are Kane, punching someone in the face might be the bond you need.

ALWAYS ON EDGE

Though Kane and I had an idea of what we wanted the book cover to look like, we didn't have a photographer. I started to do a search a few months back and found many great artists out there. They all seemed decent, that is until I saw the art of Jesse Adair. When Jesse sent us his site, I was blown away to say the least. It's unlike any other art out there. It's true, gritty, hardcore horror, yet artfully and beautifully done. I immediately sent the link to Kane. Soon as he saw it, we knew there was no one else we could go to for the photos.

A few months down the road, we were on our way to Tampa to shoot the cover. With us, we invited Amanda Loveless of Loveless FX, a talented make-up artist we met at Monster-Mania the year before. Together, we were all set to shoot one kick ass cover and some publicity photos. Beforehand though, Kane messed with my mind without even doing anything.

At this point in our working relationship, Kane has scared the piss out of me numerous times. Needless to say, I get on edge when I'm around him, waiting for his next scare. My flight didn't get in until late at night, so Kane checked me into the hotel and got me a room next to his. When I arrived I got the keys from him and brought my stuff to the room. At first, I didn't think anything of it, but after working on the book a bit, I went back to my room to go to bed. It was then that I realized that Kane had the key to the room. Knowing him, he probably went in before I got there and set up a scare.

Inch by inch I searched the room, opening drawers as if they might explode. Searching under the blankets for a dead spider, I felt myself shaking a bit as I anticipated finding something horrific in the sheets… nothing. Under the bed, he probably set up some sort of alarm that would go off under my bed and scare the piss out of me in the middle of the night. Nothing there either. Maybe he put itching powder on the towels? With a light touch, I deemed the towels safe. The old needle on the chair trick? Not a prick in sight. Oh! A severed hand in the fridge? Nothing there either. Holy crap, he didn't try to scare me. Phew!

Feeling safe in the room I double bolted the door and put a chair in front of it in case he got an extra key to sneak in during the night and blare a bullhorn or something. Drifting off to sleep I felt content that Kane wouldn't do anything. Then, at one in the morning, *thump, thump, thump.* I jumped up from a dead sleep, my heart pounding. As my head cleared I calmed myself saying it's just Kane trying to scare me. *It's not going to work!* I yelled, trying to show I wasn't scared. *Thump, thump, thump.* There it was again, was he just banging on the wall?

Flicking on the light switch I squinted my eyes from the sudden brightness as I searched the room in a panic. He couldn't be in here, no way. Jumping up I ran and looked at the door, all good. Did I miss something he put into my room? *Thump, thump, thump.* Again! It was by the window. As if I was in a horror movie I walked towards the window in slow motion. Though we were on the fifth floor I expected Kane to be floating outside of the window, looking menacing. How he would do that, I have no clue, but to scare me, he'd figure out a way. As I got closer to the window, the noise came again. To my shock and relief, I realized it was the damn air conditioner. Stupid thing froze up and was making the banging noise.

Laughing to myself I rubbed my hands through my hair. Damn bastard, Kane doesn't even have to do anything anymore and he still scares me.

SHOOTING A KILLER

On the morning of the shoot we arrived at the International Academy of Technology and Design ready to get to work. We met Jesse Adair outside and chatted a bit about what we were going to do that day. Jesse then led us into the school, where we were all pretty amazed at how nice it was. I went to a very expensive film school in New York City and it had nothing on this place. We were lead into a full function studio that Jesse had already set up. I have to say, he went above and beyond his duties. He not only built us a set, there was a craft services table and monitors for us to see each picture as he took them.

The first shots we decided to do were in front of this smoky, black background for his close up pictures. Come to find out, the singer, Sting, did a photo shoot with that very same backdrop. Jesse snapped off a few test shots and within a second I knew we were going to get some amazing photographs. The combination of Jesse's style and Kane's intense look was, for a lack of a better word, magic.

After getting a few headshots and clo⸴ ⸯ ⸠ ⸢ his face, we decided to get the money shot, th⸱ lip tattoo. For those of you who don't know it, Kane has the

125

word, *Kill!* tattooed on the inside of his lip. Personally, I'm too much of a wussy to get a tattoo, I don't like pain and I'm too fickle to decide on something to have on my body forever. The fact that Kane had a tattoo gun tear his lip apart makes me a bit queasy, but that is Kane for you. Of course he had to tell us the gory details about how the tissue split open the second the needle hit it. Ewww.

While I originally thought the lip shot would be one of the easier ones to get, it proved to be the hardest one of the day. For one thing, none of us realized how hard it would be to light the inside of someone's lip! It's so wet and shiny we got a ton of glare on it. Then to get it pulled down just right so it looked good, was a pain in the ass. It took forever, but we got it.

Photographer, Jesse Adair, Shooting Kane

Having the headshots and lip done, it was time to get the angry close up shots. Kane is a master at this. He doesn't have to do anything but look at the camera to get a mean look. I was sitting right by the camera so I could see Kane and the monitor after each shot was taken. As I was looking at the screen, examining a shot, Kane screamed to get an angry, pissed off yelling look. Always being jumpy around Kane, it sent me flying; I almost fell out of my seat. I swear, this book is going to take years off of my life.

With the headshots done, it was time to head into the make-up phase....

THE KILLER AND THE AUTHOR

After the headshots were done, we got Kane in the make-up chair. Our concept was to have Kane look like he just got in a fight to get some gritty, tough looking shots. Having always loved special effects make up, I took up a spot near Kane and Amanda so I could watch her work her magic.

Within a few seconds, Amanda had a nice looking bruise on Kane's cheek. And his eyes had been darkened. Next it was time to give him a menacing scar across his cheek. Amanda was nice enough to explain what she was doing. First she drew a line with some red make up. Then she used a chemical that is basically chloroform mixed with other ingredients. Using a tiny brush she applied it over the red line. With a hairdryer she dried the toxic substance. Within seconds, my mind was blown away; the line had turned into a scar that looked so real that even from a foot away I couldn't tell it was fake. After a bit of powder, Kane was ready for his close up and I was next in the chair.

While Kane had more pictures taken, Amanda worked on my makeup. I was given a bruise, had my lip split open with the same scar technique, made my right eye bloodshot and blackened out a few of my teeth to make them look like they were missing. Before we were to shoot I ran to the bathroom. As I started to wash my hands I looked up and startled myself, forgetting that I looked like I had the crap beat out of me. I stood there for five minutes, admiring my beaten exterior. It made me giggle with joy.

On Set of Our Publicity Photo Shoot

Back in the studio it was time for Kane to kick my ass...something I dreaded. I knew Kane was looking for the opportunity to mess with me, and this was it. One of the first shots we did was of Kane grabbing my shirt and pulling me towards him. Simple enough, though of course he has to get into the role and actually ball up my shirt and jerk me forward. At this point I was getting a bit nervous as we still had to do

Michael Aloisi

a picture of him punching and choking me. Next up we did a shot of Kane and I staring at each other's faces looking tough. Not having a drop of toughness in me, this was hard to do. With my face inches from Kane's looking into his eyes, I wanted to piss myself. His eyes are some of the scariest things you'll ever see. They are so intense that to be looking into them that close was like looking into the gates of hell. Jesse snapped off a few pictures, then, just as I felt like I was finally getting a good tough look on my face, Kane screamed. You guessed it, instead of holding tight and yelling back, I jumped up in the air, spun backwards and almost fell over. Laughing, I looked back at Kane, whose face was still showing rage, the man takes his scaring seriously.

THE KILLER KICKS MY ASS

After several pictures of Kane and me looking tough together, well, at least Kane was looking tough, we did a shot where Kane punched me. Being still photography he didn't actually have to hit me, he just put his fist against my face and pushed hard to make it look like he had just made contact. Of course Kane couldn't just lightly place his fist into my face, oh no. Kane had to push, *hard*, against my cheek. Not only did he push hard, he started to twist and grind his fist into my face. With his signature gloves on, it felt like he was rubbing sandpaper against my skin. The harder he pushed, the more I started to tip over, trying to get away from the pain. Hopefully the real pain made for a good picture as my face was contorting in despair. Though I don't think the squeals of discomfort did my reputation any better.

After several punches and shirt grabs, it was time for the dreaded choke. After seeing dozens of people get choked by Kane and feeling what it was like when he put my hand on someone's throat, I *never* wanted to actually be choked by him. Wanting to get some good pictures, I reluctantly decide it would be best for the shoot if I just let him at me. Though I'm not religious, I said a few silent prayers, hoping I wouldn't end up paralyzed. To make it look good, we decided Kane would have me pinned to the wall. As his massive hands wrapped around my neck, I felt everything in my body tighten up. When Jesse was ready, it was time for him to tighten, though I think tighten is too light of a word. Crush, decimate, destroy and obliterate are more accurate words. Having never experienced a sensation as such, my mind started to panic. Fight back? Pull away? What could I do? We were posing for pictures, Kane wouldn't really kill me (well at least until the book was done), I'd have air again soon…right?

OOOOOOWWWWWWW!!!

As he let go I gasped for air and tried to play off the fact that I wanted to run out of the room and curl up in a ball to cry. At this point I started to wonder what the hell was wrong with all the people who *want* to be choked by this man. Of course, we had to do the shot several more times. The second time I think he gripped a bit harder as I felt veins I didn't know I had bursting in my head. The longer he had his hands around my neck, the more I started to tip away from him as I could not control my body from wanting to get away. On the third take, he gripped a bit higher and I had the oddest sensation I ever felt. My tongue, for the first time in my life, moved on its own. It started to click and slap around in my mouth. The squeeze must have been right on that muscle. Needless to say, I did not like this sensation.

After four or five takes I felt my skin starting to feel raw and tired, not to mention every muscle and tendon in my neck. I had had enough and thankfully Jesse got the shot. I had survived the choke, though I think I'm emotionally scarred for life.

Next I go from being choked to having my neck sliced open...and I thought writing was supposed to be a safe profession.

SLICE OF LIFE

After getting the life choked out of me, it was time to get my neck makeup done. Though from the way it felt, I thought it was already sliced open. To make my neck look like it was slashed by a machete, Amanda started off by using some mortician's wax, molding the wound on my neck. Once she had it just right she slathered on liquid latex to make it look seamless. After drying it, she painted the wound and added, my favorite, ramen noodles! The noodles, once soaked in blood would look like snapped tendons and veins. Sick, awesome stuff!

The process took about forty minutes, and it looked amazing. Once she started splatting the blood on, I was in heaven. I have always dreamed of getting killed in a horror movie and for now, this was close enough, especially since I was going to be killed by Kane Hodder! On the set I got into place, Kane grabbed my hair and held his machete up in the air. Being that it was a real machete, I started to worry about Kane snapping and actually swinging it down on my neck. I just kept telling myself that he needed me for the book so he wouldn't do that.

After several pictures with the machete up in the air, we then took some with Kane holding it to my neck and other various poses with me about to die at the hands of the killer. With those shots taken, it was time for my death scenes. Lying on the floor, Kane sat behind me and leaned on his machete as if he was proud he had just killed the author of his book. Amanda proceeded to pour a puddle of blood on the floor. Being the sick person I am, I enjoyed having my face in a pool of redness, pretending to be dead. What better way can you spend a Sunday?

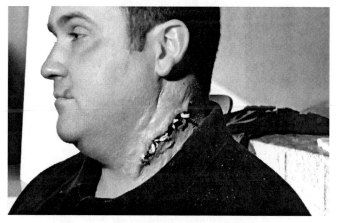

My Neck Wound In Progress

With the shots done, we were finished for the day. In the bathroom I cleaned up as much as I could, giggling to myself as I watched the blood drip all over the place. Finally clean, well at least enough to drive back to the hotel, I left the bathroom, feeling giddy that the day went well. Thankfully my good mood had me walking a bit faster as Kane jumped out and tried to grab me. Amazingly, he missed by a few inches, therefore lessening the scare. I knew he was going to try and get me at some point, and he did, though this time not as bad. Back at the hotel would be another story.

The Final Cut

STILL ON EDGE

Arriving back at the hotel, I wanted nothing more than to shower. I had dried blood behind my ear, down my stomach, caked in my hair and pretty much all over my body. Getting cleaned up was a priority. I told Kane I would meet him in a half hour so I was in a bit of a rush to get showered. I turned on the water full blast, it was steaming hot and I just couldn't wait to wash off the blood. Jumping in, it felt wonderful. I started laughing to myself as the blood ran down my body and swirled in the drain like the shower scene in *Psycho*. I was feeling good and enjoying my shower until I turned around and noticed there were no towels on the rack. *What the hell? They just cleaned my room. Why were there no towels? Damn it Kane!*

Finishing my shower I pulled back the curtain and looked around the room, no towel, and no bath mat. Nothing. Damn it! Dripping wet I stepped out, slipped on the floor a bit, grabbed the sink and regained my balance. I cursed Kane once again as I made it to the carpeted room. Stomping to the phone, I tried to call the front desk, there was no dial tone. Then looking behind the end table I saw that the phone was unplugged, that bastard. Plugging it in, soaking the floor I called the front desk, no answer. Three tries later and I finally got through. As calmly as I could, I asked for towels.

The next five minutes I stood there naked, trembling as the air conditioning blew on my wet body. When the knock on the door came I stuck my hand out and snagged the towels. Finally dry and late for meeting Kane, I stomped downstairs planning revenge for the joke he had just played on me. Charging into the conference room I blurted out, *You Bastard! You got me good this time.* He looked at me, laughed and asked what the hell I was talking about. I went on to explain the story; Kane couldn't stop laughing... because he didn't do it. At first I didn't believe him, but he promised me and swore he wouldn't do something so lame; he would have done something much worse.

Though I believed him, I still went and asked the front desk about the towels. Come to find out they washed the towels and the maid had forgotten to put them in several rooms that day. And the previous occupant must have unplugged the phone. Once again, Kane scared the shit out of me without having to do ANYTHING.

Having to work with Kane for the next year or so, on this book, is likely to give me a heart attack.

KILLER HEART

Kane has been blown up, lit on fire, burnt, crashed in cars, fallen off buildings, been in fights, hung on to helicopters and has done pretty much every other crazy stunt you can imagine. He is a man's man who can drink you under the table and still kick any man's ass in the bar. He has dirt, piss and vinegar in his veins. Crass, crude and vulgar are words that describe him best, yet... he has a heart that would make a Care Bear jealous.

Over the process of the book I have spent time with Kane and talked to him enough to learn that he is one of the nicest people I know. Kane's fans can attest to this fact. Convention after convention fans line up to meet and talk to Kane. Even ones that have met him ten times wait in line for an hour just to say hello to him. And why is this? It's the amazing combination of crude jokes, bad boy appeal and heart. As every fan shows up to meet him Kane is more than happy to offer a handshake, a quick conversation, a joke and even a hug for a picture. Kane doesn't stop there though.

Being in charge of running Kane's website, Facebook page and email for the book I filter numerous emails day after day. Most emails are from fans talking about how much they love his work or how they want him back in the role of Jason, but every now and then a touching email comes in that is more than moving. A lot of these emails are from fans that had to overcome an obstacle in their life. Kane knows more than anyone how hard it can be to overcome a tragic accident. He also knows that it is possible to come back from death's door and to be successful. Kane goes out of his way to connect with fans that are or have been in a situation like this. While a lot of these emails are private, I do want to share some of the stories I hear about the man....

One particular email Kane received a few months back was from a young lady whose mother was a big fan of Kane's. The mother had multiple surgeries that resulted in walking with a cane. She was embarrassed by this fact and of the scars that the surgery left. Kane pulled her aside and told her to never listen to anyone who made comments about her scars and that the next time he saw her, she wouldn't need the cane anymore. Using that motivation, the woman worked hard at her rehab and the next time she saw Kane, she didn't have to use her cane. Thrilled by this, her daughter wrote a very heart filled thank you to Kane, for she didn't think her mother would have done it without Kane's encouragement.

As another example, the other day I happened to stumble upon an article written by a guy that went to Monster Mania 17 that explains exactly what I am talking about. Below is the article in its entirety, which first appeared on the following website, www.WreckingHouseMagazine.com.

Kane Hodder: Truly a Class Act

I've been a fan of the Friday the 13th series and Kane Hodder for a real long time. This past weekend at Monster Mania Horror Convention in Cherry Hill, NJ Kane did something that really deserves recognition. While talking to a friend of mine David, he told me a really nice and touching story about meeting Kane Hodder. David is handicapped and is in a wheelchair. To make a long story short, David and Kane were talking and David made a reference about not being able to stand. Kane said to him "Don't ever give up and don't ever say you are unable to do anything". Then Kane told David, if you are able to stand next to me for a photo, you can have any picture on my table free of charge. David bear hugged Kane and was able to take a photo while standing next to Kane. It was a great moment. David was overjoyed while Kane remained humble. Kane is a class act. He appreciates every single fan that comes and spends their money at his table. While looking intimidating, Kane has nothing but a heart of gold and truly is one of the nicest human beings on this planet. Aside from being

141

a great Jason and stuntman, Kane is a great person. I commend him. If you ever get a chance to meet Kane, you should. He isn't there for the money; he is there for the passion and for the fans.

I could go on writing about dozens of stories like this, about how Kane visits burn camps to talk to victims and encourage them to keep on fighting, or about how Kane will have drinks with fans just to get to know them and show how much he appreciates that they *are* fans, but the best way to experience this is first hand. If you haven't met Kane, then get out and meet him the next time he comes to your town. You won't be disappointed.

DO I WANT TO BE WITH KANE FOREVER?

Never in my life have I ever had the desire to get a tattoo. There is nothing I can imagine loving so much that I want to have it on my body forever. Maybe because I'm a bit fickle and go through phases of what I like and don't like, but committing to something I could never get rid of... a bit scary. Or maybe it's just the fact that I don't like pain and the thought of having a needle rammed into my skin over and over again for hours just doesn't seem like fun. Whatever the reason is, I never, ever planned on getting one.

Having taught high school kids, I have had numerous conversations trying to talk a teenager out of getting tattoos. Especially since they are so young they might regret it later on down the road. A giant tattoo of Fifty Cent might look nice now, but in thirty years, will you still want his beautiful mug on your shoulder? I would beg and plead with them to think twice about putting something on their body that will be there FOREVER. Hell, if I got one when I was a teenager, I would have a Dawson's Creek tattoo (don't mock it, it was a great show!).

143

Michael Aloisi

I also never understood getting tattoos that you couldn't see yourself. What is the point of paying money, going through pain and then having something you can only see when you rig up five mirrors? That and I always worried about having a wrinkled, faded looking thing on my body when I was sixty. The thought of my grandkids asking what the heck is on my shoulder makes me shudder. *I know it looks like a pit bull, but it's not, that is Dawson grandson, Dawson.*

While I have always been adamantly against tattoos for myself, I have never have had a problem with other people getting them with the exception of underage kids. In fact I enjoy looking at tattoos on people, especially interesting and unique ones. Having gone to horror conventions the past few years, I LOVE seeing all of my favorite horror legends on everyone's skin.

So why am I writing about tattoos… especially if I would never get one? Well, for the first time in my life, I'm changing my mind and thinking about getting one. It could be because Kane *told* me that we should both get one before the book comes out. Not that I'm scared that he'll beat the crap out of me for not getting one, but the idea intrigues me. Ever since I was a kid I have *loved* the Jason movies. I had posters and pictures of Jason on my wall for years. Jason bobble heads and action figures were a featured art piece of my apartment in New York City (quick tip

144

for guys, horror action figures do not impress most ladies). And I have watched the films a hundred times… so what better to get than a Jason mask on my body? And if I'm going to get a tattoo, who better to get one with than freaking Jason himself? While I'm not a hundred percent sold on the idea yet, I must say, I like the idea of it.

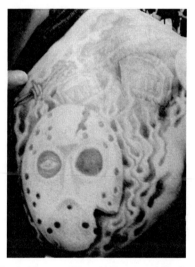

Max's Tattoo, Kane's Personal Trainer

The only question I have now is… what should the tattoo look like and *where* should I get it? If I'm going to get a tattoo, it must look amazing AND it must be hidden where it won't be on display at all times. While I'm looking forward to this idea, I'm still not sure if I want Kane to be on my body for the rest of my life.

145

ANTICIPATION ANXIETY

Last night I laid in bed and stared at the projection clock on my ceiling, watching the minutes tick by as my mind raced. The reason I couldn't fall asleep was not because of my wife snoring next to me, I'm use to that. It was the fact that earlier that day Kane and I finally confirmed that we were going to do a thirty-five city book tour.

Not only was I excited about going all over the country signing books and meeting readers… I just couldn't get over the fact that I was going to be on tour with Kane Hodder! It's funny, some days I work on the book, talk to Kane three times and think nothing of it. Then, every once and a while it hits me… the reality that I'm working with one of the most legendary horror movie stars of all time. That I'm working with a man that scared the piss out of me in my childhood. That only a year before I said my life would be complete if I *just* got Kane's autograph. And now, my name will forever be with his as the author of his biography… it's surreal to say the least.

As the minutes flew by, I thought about the different events Kane and I could do. Book stores of course, but what about screenings at movie theaters? Parties

146

at clubs? Haunted houses? Video stores? Conventions? And then of course there is the publicity… we could do radio, TV, newspapers, internet and other interviews. What outlets should we contact first? Wait, what cities should we hit and in what order? My mind started to short circuit as these thoughts fought for attention in my head. I could work on it tomorrow. I just needed to get to sleep first.

It took a while, but I finally fell asleep… a good hour and a half after I drifted off to slumber land. Only I didn't have dreams about little kitties like I normally do. Instead, I was being chased cross-country by Kane dressed as Jason Voorhees who had a giant pen instead of a machete. Every time he would catch up to me, he would try to autograph my face instead of killing me. With four months of planning the tour left to go, I hope I don't have dreams like this every night. Not that it was scary, I just spend enough time with Kane as it is, I don't need him in my dreams as well.

PUNCH ANYONE?

When it comes to punching someone, Kane is an expert. As for me, besides play fighting with my brother as a kid, I have never thrown a punch, nor been hit. This became apparent to Kane when he read the first draft of the biography. One afternoon he called me up and we started talking about different aspects of the book. As we got to one particular scene he said, "Don't take this the wrong way, but, you have never been punched have you?" At this point in our relationship, Kane still didn't fully grasp how *not* manly I am. He thought by implying that I have never been punched would make me feel like I wasn't tough (at least this is how I interpreted it), when in reality, I'm proud that I have never been hit. In fact, I'm scared as hell of getting punched. The idea of something smashing into my face is terrifying! I do not like pain, not at all my friends. I do anything and everything to avoid it. The slightest twinge of a headache and I'm popping Aleve. If there is a bee flying around, I'm running; I'm not getting stung, hell no! The point being, I avoid pain at all costs. Having gone through his burn ordeal, pain is nothing more than an annoying gnat to Kane.

During that conversation about never being, or taking a punch, Kane explained to me what it felt like. He had to make sure the fight scenes read and felt real as possible so people who have been in fights would believe them. With my non-experience, I had turned the physical reception of punches to feel phony and fake, but I didn't know better. After a long talk, Kane had schooled me on what it feels like to receive a punch. As much as he downplayed the punch, I still didn't want to receive one. I saw Kane only a few weeks after this conversation. While we were talking to someone they asked if we wanted any drinks. Having never drank alcohol in my life, I politely declined saying I don't drink, like I always do. The person then went on to ask questions about how and why I never drank and she did not understand this. This was something I'm use to so I responded with my normal answers. Kane quickly piped up and said how he understands how I could never have drank in my life... but he couldn't understand how have never gotten in a fight before. As he said this I took a few steps back, half expecting a sucker punch to come flying at me so I could feel what it's like to take a punch, you know, for the book's sake. Thankfully, no fists went flying.

After the realization that Kane might punch me one day so I could experience, I became on edge around him (not that I'm not anyway... I'm always waiting for a scare or for some joke to be played on me). That entire weekend we were together I kept my eyes on Kane's fists and my mind on high alert to move my body if need be. Amazingly, nothing happened, Kane never tried to punch me. I have seen Kane a few dozen times since then and he still hasn't knocked me on my ass... but I know one of these days it will happen... or hell, he'll find someone for me to punch in the face... not that I could do it. If the snap crackly pop of someone's neck being choked grosses me out, the feeling of their cheek and one being crunched under my knuckles might make me vomit. Of course if it ever does happen... at least I'll have a good story to write.

**Ummmmm No...Getting Punched
Does Not Seem Like Fun to Me**

THE OTHER SIDE OF THE TABLE
AT MONSTER MANIA 18

A horror convention is like Christmas to a child for a fan... it might even be better. The Monster Mania conventions are like those really special Christmases where you got the one toy you have been wanting all year long. For me, this convention was even like the best holiday ever as it was a reunion for my favorite horror movie series... *Friday the 13th*.

While I was there for business to promote Kane's book and to meet up with another of my authors, Brian Orlowski about his upcoming book, *Strange Guts*, I couldn't help but be there as a fan as well. After setting up Kane's table with all of our Kane-orbilia, I reached into my box and clutched together my copy of *Crystal Lake Memories*. Over the past two years I had gotten a few dozen autographs in the book, which for any fan is like a bible. While I was eager to talk up the book with fans, on the inside I was the kid who couldn't wait to get out of bed so he could run downstairs and rip open his presents.

They will all be here for three days... they will all be here for three days, I repeated in my head as I forced myself to stay seated and to not run to the tables of the horror

151

stars I have seen a thousand times on film, but never in the flesh. Besides, while I'll always be a fan, I had to now present myself like a businessman. Sitting next to Kane I relaxed, talked to fans and handed them cards for the book while answering questions about the release date and appearances we will be making. At this point I had done several conventions with Kane and have gotten use to this routine. Having worked with Kane for almost a year, at times I forget that he is KANE HODDER, horror legend, as I see him as a friend and business partner. Listening to several fans stammer over their words because they were so excited made me remember how crazy it is that I'm sitting on the other side of the table.

I'm Behind the Table

A skinny kid, probably in his early twenties came up to the table after waiting a long time in line. He looked as if he might faint, vomit, or both. At first I started to scooch my chair backwards in case he threw up on the table, but as I saw his hand shaking when he reached out to shake Kane's hand, I realized that he wasn't sick at all, he was just excited and nervous. Stumbling a bit over his words he told Kane that he was a huge fan. As Kane thanked him for saying that the man seemed to ease up a bit. As he did, the words poured out of his mouth, he went on and on about how he grew up with Kane's movies, how he looked up to him, that Kane wasn't just his favorite horror star, he was his favorite actor, period. For a solid four minutes this man went on about how much he loved Kane and his work. Taking a picture with Kane you would have sworn that Jesus had come down to do a rare photo op with one his faithful followers. Watching this, I realized, only a year ago that man was me.

While I might be on the other side of the table now, hanging out with my horror idols, visiting movie sets, having dinners with famous killers and having people I grew up watching calling me on a regular basis… I'll always be a fan at heart. And I'll never let that go, as it's the passion that motivates me every day.

Michael Aloisi

LAST WILL AND TESTAMENT
FOR MICHAEL ALOISI

I, Michael Aloisi a resident of Springfield, MA, being of sound and disposing mind and memory and over the age of eighteen (18) years, and not being actuated by any duress, menace, fraud, mistake, or undue influence, do hereby make, publish and declare the following to be my Last Will and Testament, revoking all previous will and codicils made by me.

This living will is being made in case of my death or disappearance over the weekend of June 10, 2011. In the event that I have a heart attack, stroke or an accident while ghost hunting at the Rolling Hills Asylum in Batavia, NY with Kane Hodder, I leave all of my worldly belongings to my wife J.Anna.

In the event that I die at the hands of a ghost, which I am deathly afraid of, I grant the right for Kane Hodder to publish the manuscript of *Kill!* In the event that I die at the hands of Kane Hodder, whether it is from murder, accident or his damn obsession with scaring the piss out of me every chance he gets, I *do not* give Kane Hodder the right to publish the manuscript for *Kill!* Especially if my heart stops beating because Kane jumps out at me and

154

barks like a dog while I'm walking through an old insane asylum in the middle of the night already scared poopless.

If my death is caused by Kane Hodder I request that I be buried with a Jason mask and a machete and that my gravestone be engraved with the following: *Here Lies AuthorMike, whose life was cut short by the brutal killer, Jason Voorhees and Victor Crowley and the B.T.K killer and Ed Gein and a few other sick bastards… otherwise known as Kane Hodder.*

One year after my official burial I request that a young, slightly insane man dig my body up during a lighting storm and then proceed to stab my corpse with an iron fence rod. Then (I don't know how to achieve this, but I'm sure the executor of this will can figure it out) I request that a lightning bolt hit the pole and bring me back to life. Once back to life I will put on the mask and pick up the iron rod and kill the young man. From there I will proceed to the nearest camp and battle a psychic teenager (note to executor of will, please make sure that the psychic is at the camp within two days after my resurrection).

In the event that I do not end up dying in the hallowed halls of Rolling Hills Asylum, and instead end up comatose from a mental breakdown caused by Kane Hodder, I request that Kane Hodder be court ordered to become my caretaker. That way he must suffer for what he did to me… wait, if he takes care

Michael Aloisi

of me he could keep scaring the piss out of me and I couldn't run away because I'd be comatose. *Note to executor of will: scratch that last request.

In the event of my disappearance, please search for me under beds, in closets and in any other sizable hiding space as I might have run off screaming to hide. At the time of the search, please bring along an extra pair of underwear for me to change into when I am found. If I am not found on the premises, please expand your search to a hundred mile radius, as I might have not stopped running until the sun came up.

If I do die because Kane Hodder jumps out at me while I'm already scared to death of seeing a ghost, I request that a one million dollar award be put up for the person who can scare Kane enough to wet his pants. In order to receive the award the act must be recorded and posted on YouTube. *Note to executor of will, I know I don't have a million dollars, or even near it, but don't worry; no one could ever do it.

Lastly, in the event of my death, I request that a paranormal team try to contact my ghost as I am determined to come back as one. If you hear the disembodied voice of a small girl sobbing, that will be me.

With Regards,
Michael Aloisi

*Note to executor of will: If I do not die and somehow live through this weekend, please destroy this letter and revert to my previous will.

HOLY CRAP...I'M ALIVE!

As I sit and write this, tears of joy are coming to my eyes, for I can't believe that I am alive! Somehow, I survived not one, but *two* nights ghost hunting in an old, creepy insane asylum. If I was doing a regular ghost hunt I wouldn't have been so worried about my life, but the fact that I was doing the hunt with the world's most prolific cinematic killer, Kane F*cking Hodder, had me wondering if I would ever see the light of day again.

It's three in the morning and I'm lying in my hotel bed after doing the ghost hunt for almost seven hours straight, being put in ridiculous situations. I am relieved it is over, yet exhausted from the late hour, but at the same time I'm hyper from the night's excitement. As I lied down to sleep, I wiggled into bed, got comfortable and began to relax now that I was safe and snug in the hotel. Then my eyes snapped open! The room was dark, I was alone, but yet I was suddenly filled with dread... what if a ghost followed me back to my hotel room? I did have a piece of the copper from the mill that Sharon, the owner of Rolling Hills Asylum (where we did the ghost hunt) gave me.... Could something be attached to it?

Jumping up I dug through my bag, found the piece of copper and stared at it... it felt like just a piece of copper... but... what if. What if a ghost was attached to it? Wait... I don't believe in that stuff... right? *Ah crap.* After flipping on the lights I jumped back in bed with my laptop and decided to write until I fell asleep. You know, because ghosts won't do anything in the light (of course I learned that is crap!). Wait a second, there could be something worse than a ghost lurking close by, waiting to pounce at me when I'm least expecting it... KANE HODDER. It was late, he was tired, but that could all be a cover. What if he was planning to come and scare me now... when I wouldn't expect it, crap. Well, I'm awake now, and probably will be for hours, so I guess I should start telling the story from the beginning.

THE WEEKEND BEGINS

Kane and I talk almost daily as we are continuously going back and forth with manuscript questions and promotional plans. A while back he mentioned a ghost hunt he booked in upstate New York. Being only a four hour drive from my house, I offered to go up and do the hunt with him… it would be great for the book after all.

The week before the event Kane and I were at Monster Mania in Hunt Valley, MD, so I didn't have much time to think about the fact that in less than a week I'd be doing something I'm petrified of. Back home, the rest of the week flew by as I was busily working on tightening up the manuscript. Before I knew it, it was Thursday. Leaving the next morning I figured I should probably look into the place I was about to visit… Rolling Hills Asylum.

Doing some searches, I felt my body grow cold… *Was I really going to go to that place… with Kane?* It was then that I saw there was an episode of Ghost Adventures filmed at Rolling Hills. After a quick download, I had the episode on my television. Flicking the lights off to add to the mood, I looked at my wife with trepidation and pushed play. Within five minutes, my heart was pounding. Ten minutes into it and I was squirming all over the couch and screaming at my wife. *NO WAY! I'm not going! I can't be in there alone with Kane. There's a seven foot giant ghost? FUDGE ME!*

Halfway through the episode I turned the lights back on and started pacing the room. Normally ghost shows might give me a few chills... watching this one felt like I was on a giant roller coaster and not strapped in. My heart slammed inside of my rib cage as if I was going around the turns of the coaster, gripping for dear life. *I was going to be in that freaky, scary, old, place by myself... tomorrow night?* Trying to catch my breath I sat on the ottoman and stared at the television. *How could I get out of this? Fake an injury, sickness?* Shaking my head I heard my wife laugh at me, ghosts freaked her out as well, but *she* wasn't going on this trip... she'd be safe and sound in our warm bed when I would be walking down empty, long, black hallways... asking for ghosts to show themselves.

No! I have to go, this will be good for the book, for the journal, I have to go! Slowly building confidence, I told myself how important it was that I should go on this adventure. I'd be fine, Kane might be a tough guy who scares people for a living, but he likes me, he would protect me... I think. Just as I was gaining confidence, a disembodied horrific sounding scream came out of nowhere on the show... my heart gave out. I laid back, grabbed my wife's hand and told her I loved her and that she should live her life if I died this weekend, for as scared as I was, I was going to do it.

The Infamous Rolling Hills Asylum

DON'T WORRY, HE'S A STUNTMAN

Pulling into the hotel parking lot in Rochester, New York, I had only six minutes to check in, unpack and meet Kane for dinner. With three energy drinks already in my system I raced inside, got my room, tossed everything on the bed, grabbed my ghost hunting kit (which was basically seventy five flashlights) and darted out the door. As I caught my breath in the lobby, Kane walked in and grunted a hello. He was set to give a lecture in an hour and a half, so we had to grab dinner right away.

Even though we were on a tight schedule, Kane always finds time to scare me. Kane, who was driving, hesitated at the entrance to the restaurant, looked at me and said *I want to show you something.* Being that this was Kane Hodder, a man who killed people for a living, this set me a bit on edge. I answered with a whispered *okay* and he drove past the entrance and turned into a big parking lot next door. As he started to look around to see if we were alone, my gut sank...*what the hell was he going to show me?*

As Kane drove further into the empty abyss of the parking lot, I wondered how severe my injuries would be if I jumped out of the car to get away. Suddenly, he stopped... and looked around again. *Did he finally go nuts? Did he have a severed head to show me?* As I opened my mouth to ask what he wanted to show me, my head suddenly jerked forward as Kane slammed the gas pedal down and we started to fly backwards through the parking lot. With both hands I grabbed onto the seatbelt, pinned my head back against the headrest and waited for whatever the hell was going to happen. As the speed rose, my grip on the belt got tighter, the fabric cutting into my palms... then it happened. The world outside of the window started to spin and blur in my vision. It was like the car was on ice as it spun completely around.. As blood was about to drip from my palms, the car jerked to a stop, facing in exactly the opposite direction than we were a few seconds before. *That's a reverse one-eighty, just thought I'd show you*, Kane said so casually he could have been talking about the weather. *Ready to eat?* Not yet able to speak, I nodded.

Later that weekend I got to see my life flash before my eyes once again... thanks to Kane's "stunt" driving. Rolling Hills was a good twenty minutes from the hotel and restaurants. During the dinner break a bunch of us on the ghost hunt headed for dinner in town. Kane and I were in one car and the rest of the group was in two other cars. With the road to town being a few mile long stretch of farmland, Kane figured this was a good time to drive on the wrong side of the road at ninety miles an hour past the other two cars. Tightening my seatbelt, I hung on tight once again, only to notice that Kane was not wearing a seatbelt…

As we whizzed in and out of the cars I laughed a nervous laugh, as I had to do something to not cry. Thankfully Kane dropped back behind the cars for a bit. Of course I should have realized Kane was just prepping for his next stunt. Now it was time to go Dukes of Hazard as Kane drove on in the breakdown lane, which really didn't exist so most of the time he was driving in the dirt. One by one he passed the cars, swerved in and out and made his way to the front of the pack again. At this point my phone was ringing off the hook as the people in the other cars were calling, begging us to stop. As we got into town, Kane settled down and drove like a normal human being. Of course it took my heart much longer to calm down. As we pulled into the parking lot I considered starting to drink alcohol for the first time… hell if I spend too much more time with Kane I might have to drink on a daily basis.

THE PRESSURE BUILDS

The first night after dinner, Kane and I headed to a local hotel and met up with Sharon, the owner of Rolling Hills. As we stood talking in the lobby I could tell within seconds how passionate she was about the location. For crying out loud the woman packed up and left California to buy an old asylum because she fell in love with it... I don't think you can be more passionate than that. She went on and on telling us stories about strange things that happened at Rolling Hills... as she did this I kept getting goose bumps and felt the hair on the back of my neck stand up. After watching the Ghost Adventures episode the night before and hearing these stories, I was ready to faint. Especially when she told us that we were all set to be locked in there that night... just Kane and me.

After talking to Sharon, Kane and I snuck into the lobby bar to kill a few minutes before we headed into the lecture. Kane ordered his usual tequila and I got an energy drink (not that I needed my heart to beat any faster that night). After taking his shot, Kane looked at me and asked when the hell he was going to see me drink. This is something I have gotten used to in my life, having never drank alcohol, and I mean never. People are always trying to get me drunk for the first time. In a way I feel like a prized virgin and everyone wants to be my first... maybe t.   not a good analogy, Kane would kick my ass i r saying he wants to take my virginity... scratch that from the record. The point being, I mistakenly told Kane that I would drink if we sold a certain amount of books. If he had another thirty-five shots in him I would be comfortable in the fact that he would forget this promise, but I know he won't, and come January next year, I'll be throwing up on my computer as I try to type up a journal entry.

With the energy drink burning in my stomach, Kane and I got up and headed into the lecture. I planned on sitting in the back and observing the lecture from afar, but as I tried to do this, Kane barked at me and told me to sit in the front with him. Having no actual ghost hunting experience, I felt a bit awkward, but it ended up being a fun lecture as Kane and I were like a Laurel and Hardy comedy team, Kane being the serious, tough guy and me, the scared, goofy one. Every time one of the audience members told a story about Rolling Hills (as most of them had investigated there before), I couldn't help but let out a yelp of fear. While it got laughs, I really wasn't trying for them. I was actually that scared of going hunting that night that I couldn't help but let eeks of fear squirt out of my mouth.

During the signing portion of the event, all the people we would be hunting with the next night kept teasing me about how the fact that I might die later that night (in a playful way thankfully). As the event wound down my stomach started to tighten up in knots. The countdown was finally over; it was time to head to the Rolling Hills Asylum.

A LITTLE ATMOSPHERE PLEASE

It was almost twelve at night when Kane and I got into the car and followed Sharon out to Rolling Hills. As the populated town dwindled down and farmland became all I could see, my gut wanted to explode. I casually sipped water trying to settle my stomach and build up nerve... and that's when I saw the lightning bolt off in the distance. *Are you kidding me?* Then the light rain started to coat the windshield... *seriously? What are the odds of that?*

As the farms zipped by, the world outside got darker and darker until finally we arrived at this ancient and ominous looking brick building. Kane slowed the car and we looked at the building. It looked creepy, but how bad could it be, it was small... so we thought. When we took a left to follow Sharon to the parking lot I almost let out a swear word. The place was huge! The asylum was more than deceiving from the front. As we turned down the street, we saw that it was at least three stories high and it went the length of a football field. So much for my hopes of having a nice enclosed space that I couldn't get lost in.

After driving the length of the building we turned down a dirt road and went behind the potential location of my death. As Kane parked the car and jumped out, I quickly dug in my bag for every flashlight and glow stick I could find and stuffed them into different pockets. When I got out and looked around, my gut sank even lower. We were in the middle of freaking nowhere! Even if I got out of the asylum alive and screaming, there would be no one around to help me. *What is wrong with me? Why did I agree to this?* I thought as I shut the door and then methodically made sure that every flashlight worked and that I had extra batteries.

Kane and Sharon started to talk about the size of the building and how there is no power in most of it. I just stood with my mouth open, staring at the place as if it was the Bates Motel and I was about to check in. I squeezed the handle of my million-watt flashlight as if it was a weapon that could protect me from the ghosts that were about to give me my heart attack.

"Alright, you guys ready? I'll show you in and then leave you guys alone; you can call me when you are ready to come out," Sharon said as if she were dropping us kids off at the pool for a summer day of fun. I wanted nothing more than to drop to my knees in a dramatic fashion and scream NOOOOOOOOO while putting my hands up in the air, but I was with Kane. I couldn't do that; I had to act like I was at least a little bit of a man. With a nervous smile I nodded and followed the two. Of course being paranoid I started to panic that I was the last one in the pack; they are the ones that always go

170

missing. At any point they would turn around and be like... Where's Mike? And I'd be gone forever... This thought made me quicken my step and walk awkwardly close to Sharon.

Entering the doors, I felt like I was going to throw up I was so nervous. Could I really do this? For crying out loud I can't go to the bathroom in my own house after watching an episode of Ghost Hunters. No matter how bad I have to go I'll stay tucked under my sheets and hold it until my wife gets up to go to the bathroom five hours later. And that's my house, not some hundred-year-old asylum... with no lights on. *Son of a bitch.* My heart was starting to flutter, sputter and spaz out like a stalling bus engine as we walked up a flight of stairs, again with me at the end of the pack. When we entered the insanely long dark hallway with a lonely wheel chair sitting halfway down it against the wall, my knees buckled. Forcing my eyes to stay at the ground, I followed them to the green room where people take breaks and crews set up. At least this room had lights on.

Though I grew to love Sharon over the weekend, I wanted to slap her upside the head that night. As she wouldn't stop telling us stories about things that happened to her or other people in the building, the stories were killing me. When she finished briefing us and caused me to wet my pants a little, we walked her back to the door we came in. She wished us luck, disappeared outside and the door was locked.

Turning to Kane, I suddenly had flashes in my head of all the kills he had done in movies over the years. Looking at him I didn't see his face. Instead I saw the hockey mask that haunted me as a little kid. *What the F is wrong with me? I just locked myself into a haunted asylum with Jason Voorhees and about a dozen other killers, not to mention a few hundred ghosts... oh and a giant seven foot ghost as well. I am such an idiot.* As I contemplated trying to break through the door behind me, I suddenly heard a noise outside. And no, I am not writing this to make it sound good, I swear to god, at the exact second we were about to start our hunt, the rain came pouring down and thunder rolled in the distance. Kane looked at me and gave a slight smile.

A MORGUE…SERIOUSLY?

As I followed Kane into the dark, long, creepy hallway, my entire body started to shake like a cold Chihuahua. Literally, I was trembling so bad I had to consciously think about slowing down my breathing. My stomach churned and tightened so badly I didn't know if I was going to throw up, crap myself, or faint. I wanted to turn and run out of the building, but it was like I was magnetized to Kane, as I instinctively wanted to follow him as to not be alone. This was going to be a long night….

The second we got away from the dull light in the doorway, my eyes started seeing things, there were ghosts everywhere, I started feeling spider webs on my back… basically, I was freaking out. It was time to pull out the big guns, my 1,000,000-watt flashlight! Flicking it on the entire hallway was suddenly illuminated; Kane stopped in his tracks and turned to me. *What the hell is that?* Kane said looking at my glowing hand. *My flashlight.* I eked out, knowing he was going to tell me to put it away. *That's not a flashlight, that is a spot light, that thing is ridiculous.* Click, the light went off.

You see, Kane is not only a badass scary guy, nothing scares him, meaning, he doesn't like to use flashlights when doing a ghost hunt. I can see sitting in a room in the dark, but Kane doesn't even use one to walk! The man is a freak of nature, nerves of steel and he can see in the dark somehow. To appease Kane I took out my glow stick flashlight, which illuminated about my fingers and nothing else and tried to use that to walk. Not only am I afraid of ghosts, I'm afraid of tripping on something too, especially in a dark old building I have never been in! How do these things not cross Kane's mind? The guy just walked in front of me like a tank plowing through the countryside.

Instead of starting off our little tour of the paranormal in some place nice and easy like say… the lobby, Kane made a B-line straight for the morgue. Yes, the place has a real morgue, as in a place where dead bodies were stored. In case you didn't read that right, I said, a MORGUE! No one should EVER go to a morgue unless you are DEAD! And of course it's not a nice shiny morgue with neon lights like in CSI, no, no, this one was pitch black and a hundred years old with a very convenient wooden sign simply saying, *Morgue. It freaking said morgue!* Who does that? Can't you have a code name to make it less creepy like, resting place for the dead? Dead lobby? Deceased dining hall? Purgatory? Anything besides morgue would do… anyway, the second we entered, what do we notice, but walk-in freezers. Old 1930's walk-in freezers with wooden doors. At first I chuckled; we weren't in the morgue! We were in the kitchen, what a relief. *Hey, they use to store the bodies in here, why don't you sit in it and I'll shut you in, see if you can get anything.* Kane's words echoed in my head, *bodies in here*, ok, so we were in the morgue... and that's a freezer for bodies.

As Kane opened the freezer door to let me walk into the icy tundra that they use to store DEAD BODIES in, something happened inside my head. With my normal tendencies to turn to a pile of Jell-O at the slightest bit of fear, you'd think I would have fainted. I was in the pitch black, in a morgue, with Jason Voorhees, who just opened the door of a freezer for me to enter, but I didn't faint. Amazingly, the cold sweat, chills and constant need to vomit, disappeared and I walked right into the freezer... I wasn't afraid, my underwear might have been a bit soiled, but I wasn't scared... what the hell was happening?

BALLS OF STEEL

Standing right where dozens of bodies use to be stacked up, I started to giggle to myself. I wasn't scared. *How was this possible?* As Kane opened up the door I smiled at him. After giving me a strange look he asked if I had experienced anything, I just said *no* and kept walking. This time though, I wasn't glued to his legs. I walked a few feet behind Kane and I wasn't scared.

Now, if I was a spiritual man or a believer in force fields or auras or Trix the Rabbit, I would have thought that some spirit came to me and let me know that I would be alright that night; that there was nothing to be scared of, but I'm not that guy. While Trix has a great cereal, I know he is not real. Instead, I just chalked up my newfound manhood to... well, I'm not really sure. Maybe the fact that for once I didn't really have a choice to be scared; I couldn't just run out screaming. I had to face my fears, and when I did, they weren't as frightening as I thought they would be.

With my new shiny steel balls in place, I was comfortable walking around with Kane through creepy places for hours on end. We sat in an old

176

church area and did EVP's, we roamed around from room to room trying to experience stuff and Kane even, gulp, left me alone. Putting me in an old patient's room, he set up his night vision camera and focused it on me and left the room, leaving me alone in the pitch black. Thinking back now, I can't believe I did it, but yet, I was fine! I wasn't scared and sadly, I did not experience anything. Actually, if I did experience anything, my new set probably would have exploded leaving me with none.

Kane repeated this method of leaving me along in creepier and creepier situations over and over again and each time I was fine. Though in the back of my mind I was waiting for Kane to be plotting some massive scare. I wouldn't put it past him to have hired some of his Hollywood special effects buddies to have rigged up a system to project a fake ghost in front of me, causing me to run out of the room and right into a wall of bloody zombies. Thankfully though, Kane gave me his word when we first entered the building that he would not scare me during a ghost hunt, ever. He had too much respect for the hunt to jeopardize it by doing something like that. While he sounded sincere and was very convincing; he was an actor after all… part of me refused to believe him, yet he stuck to his word. Well… at least while we were on the hunt that is. Of course he had to jump out at me several times at the hotel.

After several hours of hunting, Kane and I didn't really experience much, but then again, Kane never does (which is a whole theory in of itself), so we decided to call Sharon back in so she could bring out the ghosts as she knows them all... As we waited for her to come over, I wondered if my new set would last if she actually got some ghosts to come out and play.

IT'S JUST MY EYES

When Sharon came back into the asylum she was shocked that we didn't experience anything. Kane said that is how it always was with him. Everyone would see a dozen things, experience crazy stuff and Kane would be left scratching his head, as *nothing* would happen to him. People would always joke that the ghosts were scared of him, but he thinks that is ridiculous.

Sharon was determined to show us something that night and took us to the end of a long, long hallway. There Kane and I sat on some chairs, about thirty feet in front of a shut double door. The other end of the hallway had to be a hundred yards away, maybe more. While the hallway was dark, slivers of light shot in here and there from the streetlights outside. With the lone wheelchair sitting halfway down the hall by itself and the numerous dark, dark doorways along the way, it was creepy to say the least, yet I still felt pretty comfortable, especially since I was sitting and had my back to the wall.

As Sharon set up some flashlights at ten foot intervals, she told us about this area of the hallway and how much stuff they have experienced here.

Supposedly there was a ghost that would walk back and forth past the double doors behind us and sometimes jiggle the handles. I didn't like the idea of a ghost popping up behind me so I shifted my chair so I could easily look down both ways of the hall with a quick glance. As I settled in my chair Sharon went on about Roy, the seven foot ghost that liked to come out and visit her. At this point, while my newfound confidence was still there, I could feel my heartbeat pick up just a bit.

Kane sat next to me with his arms crossed, looking skeptical to say the least. The way the two of us were sitting with Sharon in front of us, it felt like we were waiting for a show to begin. And sure enough, one kind of did. Sharon leaned against the wall and started talking loudly into the air... to the ghosts. Now she is a really cool lady, but at this point I was starting to think she was a bit off her rocker. And soon as that thought came into my mind, one of the flashlights flickered on when she asked it to. This made me lean in a bit, interested. I heard Kane make a slight grunt. I'm not sure if it was a disbelieving grunt or one of interest. Regardless, I wanted to see more.

With one flashlight fully on, there was a loud creaking noise in the room next to Kane. Sharon instantly told us that it was a certain ghost who usually made noises in there. Kane and I looked at each other; I gave him a raised eyebrow. Being skeptical, I thought it was curious, but it wasn't proof to me, old buildings make noise. After a few minutes of looking into the dark doorway, I turned my gaze back to Sharon who hadn't moved and was still asking the ghosts to come out and show Kane and me themselves. Once again, as she asked them to turn on a flashlight, one started to flicker very subtly. *Come on, you can do it, turn it all the way on.* Sharon said as if encouraging a little kid to tie his own shoes. Then, sure enough, the light snapped all the way on. Hmmmmmmm....

Again, being a skeptic, the whole flashlight thing is a bit fishy to me. If I hadn't seen Sharon purchase and open the flashlights herself I might have thought they were rigged. Even so, my mind refused to believe it was ghosts doing this. If you leave a flashlight just barely off, physics states that it just *might* turn on. The wires are touching and only need the lightest touch to turn on. Of course this is the philosophy as to why spirits can turn them on; they only need a little effort. In my mind though, of course they would turn on if you leave them that way. Then again... a lot of them seemed to turn on and off when Sharon asked them to. And a few even barely lit, flickered and popped on, then right off. At this point, I was starting to believe what was happening, yet in the back of my mind I made a note to contact Mythbusters to see if they could figure out the whole flashlight thing.

After a few minutes of an interesting light show, Sharon started asking Roy to come out. Then she decided to play some music for him, as supposedly he was an avid fan of classical music. Using her iPhone she quickly pulled up some appropriately creepy music from the time period he lived and started to play it. As I took a deep breath I tried to remind myself that I was now a man and that the addition of spine tingling old music at two in the morning, in the dark, in an old asylum was nothing to be afraid of. Some more lights snapped on and off and as I turned behind me to look at the double doors, which had two tiny windows, glowed with soft light from outside. Without a word I reached out and slapped Kane on the shoulder. Whatever I was seeing I didn't want to scare away, when he looked at me I nodded at the door. In the corner of the left window I swore I saw a shadow looking out at us, and right where its feet should be, the light was blocked. *Gulp.* Kane looked for a second and they asked me what I was seeing. I explained it, never taking my eyes away. *It's just a shadow, it's nothing.* He whispered and then turned back to the front. Taking a breath I stood up and took a few steps forward, approaching the first ghost I ever saw… only to realize it *was* just a shadow from a tree. *Damn it.*

A bit defeated, I turned back and looked down the long hallway, when something caught my eye. At the very far end, in the slightly lit doorframe, I saw something. This time I didn't say anything; I wanted

182

to watch it first. Then I tensed up, my eyes grew wide and my mouth dropped open. No way did I just see that, *no way*.... Clear as day, I saw two people walk past the doorway. I couldn't see any details on them, but sure enough, two people walked in the same direction down the other hallway, past the doorway of our hallway. A bit freaked out, I shut my eyes and thought. There was NO WAY there was anyone else in the building with us. The place was locked down like fort Knox, we were locked in and it was two in the morning... we were alone.

Creeeeeeeepy Hallway

Okay, if what I saw was real, it was not human. *Ok, not freaking out just yet, let's take another look.* Looking back I figured I would see nothing, and that I would have to brush off what I saw as a fluke. Yet, when I looked back, there were more full shadows walking by the doorway. Now, remember, I'm a skeptic, yet I was sitting there staring at shadows walking around like it was a busy hospital hallway. One after another I saw one walk by. And there was *no way* it could have been shadows from a passing car, because these shadows stopped, moved like humans, and even looked as if they were talking to each other. At this point I couldn't hold in what I saw. *Kane, there are people walking back and forth down the hallway.* Kane responded by shifting in his chair a bit and looked down the hall. *It's just your eyes.* He barked at me as if I was nuts. It wasn't my eyes. I had Lasik surgery a year ago and now have *better* than 20/20 vision. I'll probably get punched for this, but Kane is a bit older than me; I'm sure he couldn't see the end of the hall as clear as I could. *No, Kane there are people walking around!* Again he repeated it was my eyes. To be sure, I looked away, rubbed my eyes and looked back. This time, there was no one walking by, maybe it was my e... *holy crap it wasn't!* Just as I was about to dismiss what I saw, a figure, clear as day, grabbed the doorframe, leaned in and looked right down at us. It took a step into the doorway, as if trying to get a better look at us, and then went back the way it came.

At this point, I didn't want to lose my new set of shiny steel balls, so for my sanity, I told myself it was my eyes, I was seeing stuff, it was late, I was tired. I think if I didn't, I might not have been able to get up from that chair until the sun came up. It wasn't until

I got home and I was telling this story to my brother did I realize that, *I freaking saw ghosts!* As I was telling him the story, saying it must have been my eyes, he told me I was an idiot and that I probably really saw something. As I thought back, and replayed the images in my mind, that is the only answer I have, it *was* ghosts. And yet, as much as I believe what I saw, the skeptic part of my mind keeps fighting it, saying there has to be a rational explanation for the disembodied shadows walking around. Just like my mind fights the fact that when we later went up into nurse Emmie's room (supposedly one of the most active rooms) and Sharon asked Emmie to show herself to us, I broke out in a heavy, heavy sweat and got extremely nauseous and almost threw up. I kept this to myself and kept thinking, it's late and I'm hungry, it must be hunger. Yet when I told this to someone else, they said that is what it's like when a spirit touches you.

Do I believe in ghosts now? No, I won't let myself. And the reason I won't is because if I did believe in ghosts, I would never be able to live a normal life. I would always be nervous, freaking out that ghosts were following me, always messing with me. I would never be able to sleep with the lights off (hell I have a hard time doing that now. I'm always scared Kane will pop out at me, even though he lives on the others side of the country!) I'd rather rationalize strange things that happen. Otherwise I'd go through a pack of Depends adult diapers a day!

I SURVIVED THE NIGHT WITH KANE…
NOW WILL I SURVIVE THE GROUP HUNT?

With my new, *I Survived the Haunting at Rolling Hills Asylum*, shirt on, I strolled out of my hotel room at the crack of… ok, well it was two in the afternoon and I was heading out for breakfast. I'm not used to being up that late; going on ghost hunts is going to wipe me out! And I had to do another one that night. Regardless of the fact that I was still half asleep, I was eager to tell all the people I met the day before that I had survived the night with Kane, something I never thought would happen.

After a quick Taco Bell breakfast, I went back to the hotel and ripped up the letters I wrote to all of my loved ones in case I didn't make it the night before. Then, I went down to find Kane, and of course… he scared the hell out of me. He said he was in the gym, but when I checked it; there was no one there. Heading down the hallway, the bastard jumped out at me with his usual growl. Like always, I jumped up in the air with a yelp while flaring my arms and legs in a dance of fear. How I haven't gotten used to this by now, I have no clue.

As my heart settled down, Kane and I drove over to Rolling Hills. Seeing it for the first time in the daylight, I could finally appreciate not only its massive size, but the fact that it was in the middle of absolutely nowhere! The group that we would be touring with later was inside on a historical tour of the building. We decided to wait outside and kill time by talking to Kelly, one of the workers at the asylum. She told us some stories about the place and went back and forth on a bunch of different things. At one point, Kelly decided to use the bathroom, which was a port-a-potty hidden back by the entrance to the building. The second the door shut behind her, Kane jumped up from his chair and stealthily darted across the parking lot. Getting closer to it, he slowed down, crept to within arms distance and then slammed both of his hands against the sides while screaming like a maniac. From inside came a loud scream followed by a furious *Mother F*cker!* Within seconds, Kane was back sitting next to me.

At the sight of the door bursting open and the red, scrunched up face of anger that Kelly was wearing I burst out laughing. Finally, for once I was not the one being scared. And I got to tell you, on this side, it was a hell of a lot more fun! Kelly strolled over and didn't believe for a second that it was me who had done that to her as Kane was suggesting. After settling down a bit, she kept swearing. I wanted to hug her, for I knew the torment her body was going through. The weak limbs that follow after the shot of adrenaline wears you out, the blood pulsing in your head from the fright and anger at being scared and the fact that you were scared for no reason; then the

187

slight giddiness of knowing that a horror legend had just scared you and you now have a great story to tell. It was all too familiar to me... and finally, I got to see it from the other side.

When the tour was over, Kane and I followed the group of twenty some odd people into the "green room" in the asylum, which is where people took breaks during ghost hunts. Kane did an informal Q&A with the group and Sharon gave an informative lecture about different ghost hunting devices. Halfway through it I was waiting for Dr. Egon Spengler from Ghostbusters to come out and show us how to use the photon guns. There were some cool, odd things that I had never used or even seen before. Meters, thermometer things, radios that talk to the dead, it was all there and more than interesting. Sharon even had divining rods, (which looked like straightened out wire coat hangers) I thought were used to find water in the old days, but come to find out can be used with ghosts as well. Watching Kane try to use them was like watching Godzilla flossing, it just wouldn't work.

With the Q&A time over it was on to the dinner break. An excited bunch of women won the privilege (or punishment depending on how you look at it) to have dinner with Kane. There were three young ladies who came down from Canada for the hunt, a young artist and several local women. Together we went to a great barbeque place and watched Kane stick a knife in his eye in-between the cornbread appetizers and our meals. I have seen Kane do this numerous times, it's a trick he loves and it never fails to get the gasps. In fact, it grosses me out so much I refuse to watch it. To my horror, as I looked to my left to not see Kane's eye come dangerously close to popping, the artist, Tabitha that was right in my vision was attempting the same trick with a fork. Once again my stomach turned as I prayed that I wouldn't be spending the night in the hospital with anyone.

After a lot of laughs and a few group pictures, the sun was setting and it was time to go back for the group hunt!

AND THE HUNT BEGINS

After listening to a list of rules and precautions, everyone was divided up into several groups and ushered off to different areas of the asylum by workers. The plan was to have Kane and I spend time with each group. As the groups rotated locations every few hours, so would we. While everyone was really excited to hunt with Kane, a buzz was starting around me. People wanted to hunt with me! As I blushed, my confidence went through the roof, that is until I realized that they only wanted to hunt with me because of the high possibility that I might wet my pants as I cried in fear. I was unknowingly going to be the comic relief that was needed during a tense hunt.

The first group we visited was in the old boiler room where a young child was supposed to haunt along with an old maintenance man. Standing in the pitch black, in a circle, with ten or so people was a new experience for me. Everyone was sooooooo serious; I was having a hard time not making jokes (which I do when I'm nervous) as people asked questions to the air. Sadly, I found that instead of focusing on ghosts, I was painfully trying not to make noise as I stood there. The ground was sandy, so every tiny movement of my foot sounded like dragging a file cabinet across the floor. Being a very fidgety person, I was shushed three times. I even apologized at one point, which received a sharp reprimand about taking this seriously... I thought I was!

Come to find out, I just happened to be standing in front of the "danger room" which was an old heavy door that leads into a concrete closet sized room with nothing in it. Supposedly a lot of stuff happens in there, hell, why don't we throw Mike in there then! After Kane tested out the room, I whimpered and went in, not being allowed the use of my flashlight. As the door shut, I couldn't see a thing. To test how dark it was I waved my hand in front of my eyes and couldn't see it. Gulp.

Trying to stand comfortably, I shifted back and forth; waiting for a drooling, rotting corpse to suddenly flash in front of my face like it would if this were a horror movie. Instead, I saw nothing. Hell, it was so dark there might have been one in front of my face, I just couldn't see it. Amazingly, I did not pee my pants, probably because I knew a lot of people were only a few feet away from me on the other side of the door. At one point I almost did though, as right behind me there was a loud thunk. It startled me enough to turn on the flashlight for a brief second, which received a loud yell from Kane to shut it off. Thankfully I saw nothing in there with me.

After a while I was freed from the room and entered back into the circle where flashlights went on and off a few times while people asked questions. While everyone talked to this child ghost, I just thought to myself, why the hell would a child be in the freaking scary boiler room? It made no sense to me, but I didn't dare speak up for fear of becoming one of the ghosts there myself.

After switching groups we moved to a long hallway that was supposed to be very active. I was handed some device that looked like an electronic meter from hell and was told to use it. Before I could ask how to, Sharon was gone. With this new group standing with me I fumbled with the switches, making it screech and squeal annoying sounds. Again and again I tried to get it right but instead I just hurt people's ears with it... so I shut it off, defeated.

Kane with His Recorder Ready

A few minutes later we moved into a large open room in the basement. Tired of standing, I quickly ran to a chair and sat down. Kane joined me and the rest of the group settled in as well. This time Sharon came back with this device, which was a small speaker that would randomly blurt out words. Ghosts are supposed to use it to communicate. The thing was creepy. Kane held it and for long stretches of time in the darkness it didn't make a sound, then suddenly it was say, "midget... roof... pain." Then it would stop for another long pause and blurt out words again. It was so random that it was hard to think it had any meaning... that is until it said "Kane" several times in a row. The chances of that happening are pretty astronomical; then again it did say "midget" about twenty times. It was an asylum though; there could have been a midget ghost.

While in that room one of the flashlights kept going on when Sharon asked it to. I snapped a picture and got my only good evidence, though I'm still not sold at all on orbs. You can see it to the right. The only reason I look at it with a critical eye is that I took it the second the light snapped on... and I did not capture any other orbs that night.

Michael Aloisi

DEAR SHARON AND THE GHOSTS
OF ROLLING HILLS. I AM SO, SO SORRY...

It is with great regret that I must write this entry...
yet at the same time, I do admit it is funny as hell. To
fully understand this entry without me having to go to
into Kane's psychology, you might want to read the
chapter *What a Pisser* in Kane's biography, *Unmasked*.
In case you haven't, let's just say that Kane has a...
well he is sort of... he is like a dog, he likes to mark
his territory. Why is still a mystery to me, but I have
gotten use to the man urinating in odd places, even if
it does stress me out to no means.

Another preface to this story is a bit personal, but
necessary to my defense in the case that follows. I
have a tiny bladder. More so, I have a nerve issue
with my body, its complicated, but my nervous
system is a bit messed up. It results in my nerves
telling me I have to pee when my bladder is only half
full. Mix that with the fact that I drink about two
gallons of water a day and it means I pee on average
of 24 times a day, seriously. It's so bad that I actually
monitor my water intake on days that I will be away
from a bathroom so I don't have to go. At best, I
can't go more than two hours without a bathroom

194

break (try driving a road trip with me). With that said, the story begins.

The first night we did the ghost hunt alone, I made sure to go to the bathroom before I entered the asylum. Kane did not. No more than five minutes into the hunt, Kane told me to hold on, he had to piss. I silently prayed that he was going to make us run up stairs and go outside to the port-a-potty, but no, being down in the old kitchen he found a sink and did his business while I nervously looked around, hoping he wasn't pissing (no pun intended) off a ghost. While I was uncomfortable and nervous about it, at least it was in a sink.

As the night progressed I was happy that I had a long drive that day and hardly drank any water, for while I had to go again, I could hold it more than normal. On the other hand, the beers Kane had at the bar before must have been getting to him. As we walked through one of the long hallways doing our hunt, Kane suddenly veered into a room and right into a closet. Still a bit scared I followed closely behind thinking he saw something. Seeing me over his shoulder he told me he had to piss, which instantly spun me around in the other direction. When the realization that he was about to piss in a closet broke into my mind, I spun back around and protested in a high pitch voice. *Kane! That is a closet, let's go outside!* I begged ten octaves to high. Before I could finish I heard the splashing sound. My gut rolled a bit as the thought of what he was doing, freaked me out....

Thankfully, the rest of the night his bladder was empty. Mine wasn't however and I had to wait until Sharon came and unlocked the door to run out to the port-a-potty to take a much-needed leak. When the night was over I tried to block out the fact that Kane had pissed in the closet, in fact, I didn't even think about it until the next day... During a break after Kane's Q&A with the group, we decided to take a walk around the asylum as we hadn't seen it during the daylight. It was tricky, but we snuck away from the group and explored on our own so we could talk. Kane and I don't get much face time together so we tried to use as much of it as possible talking about the book and tour plans. We went up a few floors and chatted as we checked out different rooms. Suddenly, Kane told me he wanted to check out the closet, before I could realize what he was doing, he was in the closet, taking up his stance. The whole purpose of this break was to go to the bathroom, IN THE BATHROOM, not another closet! A sudden wash of fear waved over my body and I started to shake, worrying that someone might walk in, which is odd since I wouldn't be the one getting caught. When I heard voices in the distance down the hall, I tried to warn Kane but no voice would come out;, I was frozen with fear. The fact that I have never done anything really wrong in my life is probably due to this fact, the fact that I freeze up and freak out at the slightest sign of getting in trouble. Before I knew it, stuck in my position, Kane walked past me, looking at me like I was nuts for not moving. It took a while for me to relax, but I eventually did. But for some reason, the idea of someone discovering the puddle of piss never occurred to me.

Flash forward to ten hours later when it was one in the morning and I had to go to the bathroom myself. At this point in the hunt we were about an hour and a half away from the bathroom break where Sharon would unlock the doors and let people out to use the port-a-potty. It had been two hours since the hunt started and my bladder was screaming. It was time to switch groups and Kane and I were lead up to the top floor of the building where the staff used to live. We were left in a bedroom to wait for the group that would be up in five minutes. I was starting to do a pee pee dance when I complained to Kane that I had to go to the bathroom but didn't know if I could as Sharon didn't want to let anyone out during the hunt, that and the fact that I'd have to walk down four flights, find my way out, get it unlocked and then go to the bathroom and find my way back. As I rambled on about the horrible predicament I was in, Kane cut me off and said, *Yeah, I have to piss too, watch the door.* Knowing the group would be there any minute; I freaked and ran to the door to guard it as Kane went towards the closets. The room we were in actually had two closets that faced each other with a window in between them. Kane opened up the one on the

197

left and started pissing away while I panicked and guarded the door with my life. Thankfully there was a long hallway in front of the door so I could see if anyone was coming from a distance.

As Kane walked back over to me he said, *go ahead, take a piss I'll watch the door.* I laughed out loud, there was NO WAY I would ever do anything like that. Just as I said that, my bladder screamed at me, as it wanted to be emptied. *I'll just run downstairs.* I eked out to Kane, while in my head I tried to figure out how to find my way out. *Just go in the f*cking closet, I'll go in the hall and stop anyone from coming down.* It wasn't a request, it was a demand. I let out a small nervous laugh, no way, no way… but then I found myself walking towards the closet on the right. *What was I doing?* As I opened the door and stepped in, Kane took up post in the hallway. *What was going on with me? I couldn't do this.* Then, as if I was possessed (at least I'd like to think I was as this is something I would have NEVER done in my life), I unzipped my pants….

It has to be just the right combination of an unbelievably painful full bladder and the fact that I wanted to prove to Kane that I could be daring, that I could do something wrong, but whatever it was… I started to pee. When the second the stream came out of me, the guilt and horror of what I was doing crushed my soul, but it was too late to stop, my body wanted the pee out! As it flowed, I closed my eyes

198

and whispered into the air, *I'm so sorry ghosts, please forgive me, please forgive me.* When I heard Kane talking to someone in the hallway, I literally almost fainted on top of the puddle. In the distance I could hear, *I think Mike's down the other side of the floor, let's go get him.* Kane was covering for me, protecting me! Finishing up, I closed the closet, apologized to the ghosts and the building one more time and silently found my way out of the room.

In the hall I ran back into Kane who made sure to say he was looking for me since he was in front of some of the workers. I nervously said I was wandering around. We chatted for a minute then the two ladies went down to find the other group that was coming up. Now alone, Kane turned to me with a devilish smile. *I can't believe you did that!* He said almost accusingly, instantly making me feel even more guilty of what I had done. I put my head down in shame like a scolded school child and wished I could take back what I had just done. As I heard the next group coming up the stairs, I finally realized... *Dear God! They are about to investigate these rooms, what if someone opens the closet?!* To keep from falling to the floor in fear, I leaned against a wall for support. It was a muggy night and the top floor was stuffy and hot as hell, with the added nerves coursing through my body, I was suddenly soaked with sweat.

Thankfully, the group went the opposite way from the room to the far end. It didn't stop my nerves though, for Sharon showed up with a straightjacket (read the next entry for more on the jacket). To put it on, we went into the piss room. Thankfully we stayed far away from the closet. With it tightly on and snug to my body, the sweat was now pouring down my face with no means of wiping it away. I felt like an idiot as no one else was sweating like me. If they only knew it were the nerves they might have understood! When we walked out of the room to show everyone I was now in full mental patient gear, the group had come out of the far room...and my worst fears came true as the entire group of eight or so people walked past me, laughing, on their way to the room that had closets full of piss.

The Dreaded Closets Facing Each Other

I didn't want to walk after them. I wanted to run out of the building screaming... realizing this was not a good idea while stuck in a strait jacket, I took a few deep breaths and followed behind, trying to act like nothing was wrong when I entered the room behind them. The second I crossed the doorway I quickly scanned the room to assess where everyone was... thankfully no one was near the closest. The room itself had an old hospital bed, two bureaus and a few chairs. One guy was lying on the bed, Kane was in a chair and everyone else was standing. Fearing that I might faint, I waddled over to the dresser next to Kane and hopped up on top of it to sit. I wanted badly to wipe the sweat from my eyes, but my damn arms were so secure to my body I could not move a freaking inch. A rapid session of blinking and a few quick huffs of my breath was the best I could do to clear some sweat. At least no one could see that my hands were trembling.

Sharon took the lead and gave some information about the room and the man who used to live there... who also died there. When the story was over the group started to do some EVPs and ask questions to the air. Secretly I was hoping that the slamming of my heart in my chest would not be picked up on the microphones. Looking over to Kane, I almost screamed. The bastard was cool as hell. No sweat on his face, not a trace of worry crossing his brow, nothing. I wanted to kick him the face for putting me in this situation, maybe then he would show some concern… of course it's Kane. If I kicked him in the face he'd probably wouldn't even flinch and then send me flying across the room with the flick of a finger.

After a few agonizing minutes of waiting for everyone to leave the room as I watched, pretty obviously, the closet doors, trying to will people to stay away from it, I started to faint. It wasn't the heat that made me light headed; it was the guy's hand slowly reaching for the knob on the closet door that Kane had pissed in. Now, my memory is a bit fuzzy on the actual moment his hand hit the knob, maybe I did pass out, because my vision got blurry and my head hit the wall behind me. As the door swung open I thought about jumping up and running out of the room, maybe everyone would follow me. Or maybe I should just let myself faint to the floor. That would distract them from going in the closet. Regardless of my ideas, I was too weak and frightened to do anything but watch in horror as the guy snapped on his flashlight and aimed it right at the floor….

When I saw the guy's head tilt in curiosity of what was on the floor, I knew it was all over. I couldn't stop watching him, it might have been obvious, it might have given me away, but I could not for the life of me look away. The guy's face puckered as he raised the flashlight to the ceiling, looking for the source of the puddle. Then back down, up again, then back down. He even stepped in closer, took a sniff and jerked his head back. He was baffled, but he was keeping it to himself. Maybe he would just close the door and walk away… please God, please. "What are you looking at?" Someone said, exploding my tiny bubble of hope like an atom bomb. "Not sure, there is a puddle in here." Now I don't swear, but in my head at that moment I was saying a four-letter word that begins with F over and over again. "Oh God, don't tell me I have another leak," Sharon cried out. She had a leak all right, just not one from the roof.

Within a microsecond, everyone but Kane and I were huddled around the door to check out this "liquid". A dozen flashlights were suddenly lighting up a giant yellow puddle.

It couldn't have come from the ceiling, it was dry… it had to be… it stank! It's piss? No way! It is, it smells… horrible. Was it an animal? No, that's not piss, it's too cloudy to be, it's like goo. It does look thick. Maybe it's ectoplasm? No. It has to be urine. What sort of animal could have done that? It's way too big for a rat, maybe a raccoon? No, I think its ectoplasm. It is sort of gooey looking. We have had animals in here. How would it have gotten into the closet, its shut? Would someone have pissed in the closet? No way! These along with chatter of a dozen other theories, ideas and conspiracies rumbled through the crowed. All the while I sat, sweating more than I have in my entire life, riding the edge of consciousness. My heart slammed so hard that I am positive that if I were ten

203

Michael Aloisi

years older I would have had a heart attack. Kane sat
next to me still cool as could be. He even yelled out,
Come on! Who would piss in a closet, that is ridiculous. He
is an actor after all, and playing the part, he got up,
walked over to closet and looked in. *That's piss! Holy
shit. That's disgusting, who the hell would do that?* If my
hands were free I would have gotten up and awarded
Kane a much deserved Oscar.

As a tiny bit of vomit crept its way into the back of
my throat, a woman in the group realized there was
another closet behind them… the closet I took a pee
in. As she opened it I made a promise to myself to
never listen to Kane again, to never crumble under his
pressure as my heart could only take stress like this
once in a lifetime. *OH MY GOD!* The shriek was
followed by a dozen more and all the flashlights in the
room focusing on the new found puddle. More
conspiracy flew around the room, and one brave sole
stepped in and took a deep whiff of it, gagged and
almost threw up. For a split second I was offended
that he thought my piss smelled so bad, but the fear
of getting caught quickly swept back into my brain,
pushing me to the edge of consciousness once again.
At this point I was the only one in the room to not
have looked or said a word, so I spoke up. *Come on!
Really?* I eked out like a four year old lying about
wetting his bed when the thing was clearly soaked. I
slid off the dresser, my legs wobbled but kept me
erect and I walked over to take a look at my own
puddle. It was big and oddly it did look thick, though

204

how anyone would think it was ectoplasm I do not know. I made a comment about how disgusting that was then had a genius idea. *Speaking of pee, I really, really have to go, are we taking a break soon?* I lied and asked Sharon. It was brilliant, if I had to pee, it couldn't have been me who did it... right?

Five minutes later, still in the strait jacket, I was downstairs with ALL of the groups in the green room. Sweat dripped off my face at an embarrassing pace. I made comments about how hot the thing was even though it was no more fabric than a shirt. A few of the girls from Canada who I had become friends with helped me take the thing off as I did my pee pee dance and talked up how much I had to pee. By this point, the entire place was talking about the mysterious liquid that was in the two closets up stairs. Before we were allowed to take a bathroom break, Sharon took the floor and gave a very, very passionate speech about how if someone had pissed upstairs, that it was disgusting, vulgar and not tolerated. That she was going to have to clean the mess up and that if she ever found out who did it they would be banned from the place forever (Jesus, I'm so sorry Sharon). As she went on, another group spoke up and told her that another closet up stairs had the same puddle (the one Kane pissed in twice the day before and in the morning). At this point, talk of the puddles was on par with the Kennedy assassination conspiracy. People wanted to point fingers, others thought it was ghosts and some thought it was animals. All the while I kept up my pee pee dance and ran out of the room when we were dismissed. Racing out of the building I made a horrible show of how I had to be the first to go and burst my way into the port-a-potty outside. With the line forming outside of the door I suddenly freaked out, I didn't really have to pee, they'd hear that! A few tears slipped out of my eyes and I pushed my bladder harder than I ever had, squeezing every drop I could out of it to make it sound like I had to go, all the while sighing heavily, hoping it would mask the small sound. Finishing, I left the john and made jokes about how good I now felt. I must have looked like a freaking idiot. How or if anyone fell for my act... I'd be amazed.

As I stood outside chatting with people, all they wanted to talk about was the one thing I never wanted to hear a word about again... *what was that liquid?* One woman even went on about how odd it was, for when we were all at dinner she was sitting downstairs with one of those ghost radio box things that scanned through channels. It kept saying over and over again: *Water, upstairs, water, upstairs, hurry.* The ghosts were trying to tell her there was something up there! How amazing is that! Especially since we both didn't take the leaks until five hours later...

The rest of the night, all I could think about was getting caught or how I would act if someone asked me if I did it. Amazingly, no one did. Kane and I even had a talk with Sharon alone about how horrible that was that someone did such a thing. I just stood shaking my head as Kane was so believable I almost forgot that it WAS HIM... and me. When we left that night, I exploded into laughter the second we pulled out of the parking lot... Kane joined me as he knew exactly what I was laughing about. That sad part is I know Kane enjoyed it so much because he knew how much it killed me to do it in the first place, let alone getting caught.

We never did get caught and I doubt anyone even suspected that it was us... guess the secret is out now. At least I don't have to live with the guilt of it now! And to Sharon and the ghosts of Rolling Hills, I really am sorry. If I ever go back there, I'll help clean up anything you need and I PROMISE to only pee outside!

Michael Aloisi

WEARING A STRAIT JACKET
IN A HAUNTED ASYLUM…
JUST ANOTHER NIGHT WITH KANE

With everyone having fun watching good old Mike's nerves get rattled, Sharon had the, oh so wonderful idea of putting me in a strait jacket. Seems she happen to have one on hand from their haunted house the year before. Sharon and I snuck upstairs and went into a room (which happened to be the pee room) to put on the straight jacket. Why I agreed to do this with no reservations, I have no clue, but I put out my arms and slipped on the jacket. Crossing my arms, I thought to myself how the jacket felt a bit too natural…

After several minutes of tugging, tying and wrapping of strings, we couldn't figure out how to get the thing on correctly. We needed help and who better to ask than a crazy man… so we got Kane. As the sweat started to build on my head, the reality of what I was doing started to sink in. Here I was, standing in the dim light from a dying flashlight, standing in an old insane asylum that was haunted, being strapped into a strait jacket by Kane Hodder… what the hell! I was snapped out of this thought when Kane started tugging the straps behind me, tossing me back and

208

forth like a rag doll. As my arms got pulled tighter to my body I realized Kane was making damn sure I never got out of that thing. After a few more violet jerks and tugs, Kane said it was good enough and gave me a rough shove. I don't know how many of you have had strait jackets on, but the fear of falling without having the use of your arms... not fun.

How Do I Get Myself Into These Things?

With my arms securely in place, I was then paraded in front of the groups so everyone could laugh at the scaredy cat in the strait jacket. Of course, seeing me in it was not enough, oh no. Everyone wanted to leave me in the most haunted room alone. Sitting *alone* in creepy nurse's room alone was scary as it is, being in the pitch black, and NOT being able to move my arms... give me a break! Yet, when I was asked to do it, I agreed. Kane set up his night vision camera on me, they put out a flashlight for the spirits to turn on when I talked to them and left me alone in a chair. As they shut the door my eyes adjusted to the darkness, but I could still hardly see. Alone, I waited for the horrible sense of fear to wash over me like it normally does. For a split second I realized if I did get really spooked and tried to run, I'd just end up slamming into the door, as I couldn't open it. This thought did not make me comfortable, yet I felt fine. The heat was driving me nuts, but I was not scared at all. In fact, I was a bit bored. After throwing out several questions to no response, I almost fell asleep.

When everyone came back, they were excited to hear what happened to me as they all had experienced stuff in that room... I felt bad saying, *nothing*, but I had to. Of course excuses were thrown about as to why nothing happened to me... the fact that the room might not be haunted was not one of them. As I got up, no one offered to let me out of the jacket, so I was doomed to walk down three flights of stairs without the use of my arms, in the dark... what fun that was.

After being left in several other situations with the jacket, I was finally allowed to take it off and get some air. It was a relief to have it off, yet people still wanted to throw me in situations to make me uncomfortable... and I did them all. Sit in the old nursery, in a rocking chair, next to the crib with creepy baby dolls in it, check. Stay in the old surgery room, check. Alone in the old library type room, check. Even the old bathtub that they used to shock people in and the big shot ghost hunting show people wouldn't go in, check. One horribly scary situation after another, I did it without a problem. Either something at that place made me really comfortable, or I'm just not as much of a scared little girl as I thought I was. Regardless of the situation, I survived my trip to Rolling Hills.

Michael Aloisi

FINGER LAKES BURN CHARITY WALK

The day after our ghost hunt, Kane and I attended the Finger Lakes Charity Burn Walk with our friends Nate (a burn survivor) and his parents. Nate and his family have been good friends of Kane for some time and I had the pleasure of getting to know them during my journey with the book. Having the chance to get to do a walk with them was great as we got the time to meet Nate's girlfriend and talk during the three-mile walk.

Before I started Kane's book, I didn't know anything about burns besides what I knew from the few tiny ones I had when I use to cook. The idea of having more than a quarter size burn was unthinkable. I had never met anyone with severe ones or even thought about them more than watching a Freddy movie. After my research and talks with Kane, I realize the absolute horror and pain that is involved with severe burns. That day, seeing dozens of kids and teens with severe, severe burns over all different parts of their bodies... I felt horrible. Horrible that I was one of those jackasses for years that would stare and whisper to a friend to look if I saw a person with severe burns. When I was younger, when I didn't know better, a person that looked different, wasn't a person who

212

suffered a trauma, they were someone who looked different. Knowing and understanding how horrific suffering a burn really is, changed my view incredibly.

Seeing young kids run around, happy and playing with burn scars all over their legs and even faces made me want to help them, for I now knew how hard it must have been to go through and how hard the rest of their life would be with the scars they must bear. During that walk, Kane and I talked about what charity we could team up with to help kids like these and not only that, to help with burn prevention safety. By the time it was over, we finally decided to team up with Scares that Care (more about them at the end of the book).

Kane at the Charity Walk

Michael Aloisi

With the walk over, Kane and I had to rush off to finish some work. Later that day on my drive home, I couldn't help think about how hard live must having gone through such a trauma. I have psoriasis, which is basically incurable dry skin. It's on my hands, knees and elbows. While the spots are noticeable, they are small and yet I get asked ALL the time what was wrong with me. It's a pain, embarrassing and hard to deal with at times, yet it is not a fraction of what some of these kids have to go through, especially with burns on their faces. And yet they seem to have more courage and confidence than myself. It's impressive to say the least, for I have no clue how I would handle something like that.

While I have not experienced severe burns and hopefully never will, by writing Kane's biography, I feel the need to help survivors and try to prevent burns. It opened my eyes to something so horrible that I never paid attention to. Thankfully with our teaming up with Scares that Care, Kane and I will be able to help out people for a long time to come.

ON THE EDGE

Kane happened to be in my hometown recently while one of his sons was at a lacrosse camp. While we didn't have much time to get together, we did meet up one night. Instead of taking him to a fancy local restaurant or showing him the fun sights around town, I took him and my wife to a hundred year old paper mill.

For over thirty years my father has worked at a paper mill that was built in the mid-1800s. The plant no longer produces paper but the offices are still in use. With my dad working there my entire life, I have grown up going there to visit him at work. To say it's creepy in parts is… an understatement. Of course the offices are great and clean, but the old production floors are made of crumbling old brick, covered in gooey chemicals from a hundred years of production… and they all now sit silent. I wanted to show Kane the location as it would be amazing for a movie production and even a ghost hunt as people have died there in the old days when safety was a second thought.

While bringing Kane into a place where he could not only scare me, but also mess with me was not a good idea, why I didn't think of this ahead of time, I have no clue. While Kane was decent for most of the tour, he did play some tricks and touch some things that gave me a heart attack as it might have caused something to fall on all of our heads, but he behaved for the most part... I just realized that I'm talking about him like a small child, *Kane was a good boy!* Sad, but it's sort of true. Sometimes being with Kane is like being with a twelve year old Dennis the Menace.

Things were going fine until I had the stupid, stupid idea to bring Kane to the roof to show him the view of the river. Why I did not think of how dumb it was before hand, I do not know. The second we were on the roof I remembered that it wasn't the safest of places as it was flat with no edge, just a sheer drop of six floors to the cement...that and the actual roof was ancient and could cave in at any time. The second I heard the first moaning crack come from our footsteps, my stomach did a flip. *Maybe we should just, uh, look from here.* I meekly said as I stood by the entrance, what did Kane do? He made a b-line right towards the edge, the edge that could crumble under him at any second. *Kane! Don't go to close!* Of course Kane ignored me and laughed as he walked to the edge and stuck his toes over it. While I was nowhere near the edge, I started to get dizzy and feel sick. *I just wrote this guy's biography, and now he is going to die! He is going to fall, the book will never come and I'll go to jail for manslaughter... oh yeah, and Kane would be dead.* I thought as I watched him, with his hands in his pockets, toes over the edge looking at the moonlight on the water. When he asked my wife to come closer and take a look over the edge, my worlds started spinning. I screamed and yelled at her with anger, which I never do to tell her to not go any closer.

Kane stayed in place and laughed as J.Anna headed closer; I was frozen with fear. I reached out and tried to grab her, to stop her, but I couldn't. Thankfully she got close, but not too close. Kane then decided to take a walk around the roof. To his joy and my horror he saw that two of the buildings where close enough that you could jump over the gap to the next one. It was probably a four-foot gap, but still, if you didn't make it, you'd fall down six stories, hitting the walls on the way. Kane, without even thinking, leapt over it. I believe I might have blacked out for a second at this point.

Using the railing and tiny bridge, I crossed the gap and begged Kane to come back down stairs. Instead, he posed and made me take a picture of him basically hanging over the far ledge. I did it in hopes he'd be happy and want to come back down. He wasn't done yet though. No, not at all. Walking back over to the other side he jumped the gap again, though this time he turned to me and told me to do it. I laughed and said he was insane. Then, with the freaking odd power he has over me (which I really think is just the pure fear he distills in my soul), he demanded that I do it... and I obeyed. It was only a few feet after

217

all... right? Backing up I ran like an Olympian and jumped hard and far as I could, even if it was just a few feet. Of course after I landed I snapped out of my Hodder Haze and wondered why the hell I just did that.

With my entire body tingling, I wanted nothing more than to leave the roof, though Kane wouldn't let me. He walked back over to the edge, turned around and then told me that he would not leave the roof until I got close to the edge as I could. *%*$$*##* ME!* I'm not scared of heights, if I have a railing. But with nothing but a sheer drop to cold, hard concrete and nothing to hold on to, never mind the fact that the roof might cave in, I wanted nothing more than off the roof (the proper way that is). Kane pointed out a crack in the roof and said he wouldn't leave until I past the line. It took me a solid five minutes and a lot of shaking, but I did it, I crossed the line. As I waited for the wave of accomplishment to wash over me, it never came, the need to get off of the roof stayed... thankfully I was now allowed to leave.

I want to hate Kane sometimes, but for some reason, I never do. No matter the stress he puts on my heart or the things he makes me do, I keep doing them. I don't know what it is, maybe I like the adrenaline I get or the fact that I'm doing things I never would, but the truth is, I can't stay mad at this mad man... though the one day I finally lose a limb that might change.

THE KILLER AND I…ON TV?

While working on promotions for Kane's book we threw around some ideas with a few producers to do a documentary based off of the biography. While it was a good idea, it didn't come to fruition. Frustrated and wanting another way to promote, I started thinking. Then one night as I was lying in bed thinking of Kane like I always do (not that way), I thought… what about a reality show? People already love how Kane and I interact with each other, why not tape it?

The next day I sat down and worked out a pitch for a show based off of this very journal. It would be the best "odd couple" theme ever; the tough as nails famous horror movie star and the scared, timid writer setting out cross-country on their book tour. We'd film everything and show the world the crazy crap Kane made me do. I threw together a bunch of ideas about things we could do besides just the appearances; Kane making me get my first tattoo, having me drink for the first time ever, get in a fight and other crazy things I have never done but is common place for Kane. We'd even go on ghost hunts now and then and do all sorts of crazy things. Hell, I'd watch a show about my favorite horror movie star messing with a writer, maybe other people would as well.

I was thrilled when I pitched the idea to Kane and he loved it. He gave me the go ahead to pitch it to some other places, so I started doing some research. The only problem was, I had no experience in reality television. Still, I read a lot of stuff about it and reached out to some contacts. Then I came across Andrea Albin, who you might know as a writer for Bloody-Disgusting and other horror outlets. Kane and I met her on the *Hatchet II* press tour the year before. I happened to email her about doing an interview for the book and we started talking about the show. Come to find out, she runs a management company and has dealt with reality in the past. We talked about the show and she fell in love with the idea. A week later we had teamed up and she was pitching it to every company out there.

Another week later we were getting so much interest we realized we had to film a teaser piece for the show. At the last minute, Andrea and I decided to head to Jacksonville, FL to film Kane and me at a tattoo festival. Before I knew it I was getting off the plane and heading for a weekend that was...well, for a lack of better words, annoyingly fun.

I HATE KANE HODDER

As much as I love the a-hole, I hate Kane Hodder, well, certain times at least. Arriving in Florida was one of those times. Andrea picked me up from the airport and we went to the convention right away. We met up with Kane at his table and talked for a few minutes. Kane had gotten a room cheaper for me so he checked me in before I got there and gave me the keys as we chatted. Tired and wanting to freshen up, I told Kane I'd be back and headed to my room. Andrea said she'd check in as well and would go with me. After she got her key, we headed up since our rooms were near each other. When I got to my room she asked if she could come in and talk. I thought this was odd, but agreed.

The second we got in the door she said, *Oh, I need to get some stuff from the car, go with me would you?* This was odd as well, why would I go with her to her car? Regardless, I said I would but I needed a minute to unpack a few things. One of my odd OCD things is that I have to unpack the second I get into a hotel room, no matter how tired I am or how late it is, or even if someone was with me. Andrea, not knowing this protested and said we should go to the car, but again I told her to hold on. At this point I was

221

getting a bit suspicious.

Walking into the bathroom to put my toiletry bag in there I flicked on the lights and was surprised at how dark it was as only one light came on. Hmmm. I started to search the walls for another light, nothing. Then I stepped on the carpet and heard a loud crunch. *Son of a bitch.* I knew it; I should not have let Kane check me in. That is why Andrea wanted me to go with her, to get her camera so she could catch me finding Kane's pranks on film! Feeling the carpet some more, I was suddenly horrified at what might be under it, so I yelled for her to come in there. We both refused to lift it so I kicked it over to find a pile of pistachio shells and M&M's…. Kane. Then I realized that there wasn't another light switch; Kane had unscrewed all the lights. Laughing, I screwed them all back in and left the room thinking how stupid that was. Little did I know there were 17 other pranks set up for me, pretty much all of which I would fall into in the next five minutes.

Still determined to unpack, and for some reason not thinking there would be any more pranks, I grabbed the remote to move next to the bed, only I didn't get half a foot with the thing. As I slid my hand around it, I felt the slime, it was so gross I yelped and tossed into the air. Instantly, I turned and ran to the bathroom to wash off the goo. Pushing the handle up I found another layer of gunk. Determined to rinse my hand, I pushed it all the way up, though no water came out... then the sink exploded, spraying water all over me. Now wet and annoyed, I grabbed a towel to wipe my face and hands off... only to find that the towel has a huge poop smear on it. Screaming, I threw it to the floor and raced out of the room, confused and not sure what to do.

Sadly, I was forced to wipe the goo off on the bedspread. As I calmed down a bit, I opened the refrigerator to put my water in it, only to have a liter of water come flying out at me. The freaking bastard set up a bottle with a rubber band so it would shoot out at me. It soaked the floor, worst of all, later that night I forgot about it and walked through the puddle in my socks... nothing is worse than wet socks. Going back for a towel, I found that pretty much ALL of them had giant poop stains on them (I found out after that Kane has this joke stuff he buys that looks and smells like real poop that he used... at least that is what he said). Frustrated, I went to the phone to call and ask for fresh towels, only to find out that the phone would not work, he rewired the damn thing. The TV didn't turn on either and come to find out, under my mattress were light bulbs that were supposed to pop and scare me when I laid down. The pens didn't have any ink in them; the closet door handle fell off. The toilet? The seat was unscrewed so it fell off when I touched it, the toilet paper fell off the roll and flusher didn't work (I used the lobby bathroom the entire weekend). Worst of all later that night when I went to take a shower, there was no showerhead. I found it hidden in a drawer, though it still hardly worked as he filled it with the same Vaseline he covered the remote in. The only time I got to laugh was when Andrea and I decided to actually go to the car to get the camera, as she went to leave and grabbed the door handle; she was the butt of one of these jokes as it was covered in more Vaseline.

Stare Down...Guess Who Wins

Knowing Kane had to be dying to hear how everything went I called him up and asked him if he wanted anything before I headed back down. He asked if everything was alright with the room, so I said, *yeah, it was great, why?* I kept up the joke when I got back to his table and saying that I didn't want to be on the second floor so I asked the front desk to move me to a higher one, which they let me do. I saw a slight panic in his face as he realized the maid would find all the stuff and he'd be paying for it, but I couldn't hold a straight face long enough. At that point I was able to laugh at what a jackass Kane was. Come to find out he set up 20 things in total (3 of which I hadn't found yet) and it took him a few hours to do it all. He even went out to CVS to buy crap to mess with me… that is how dedicated this man is to playing jokes on someone.

Of course the jokes didn't stop there. He jumped out and scared me with a fog horn, followed me into the bathroom and literally scared the piss out of me while I was taking a leak, and worst of all, when I went to bed that night, he sprayed five squirts of his "Fart Spray" under my bedroom door, making my room smell like a sewer. One of these days I'll get him back, I just don't know how… well, that and I'm scared as hell that if I piss him off, he'll get me back, much, much worse.

As much as I want to hate Kane Hodder for making my life hell, it's too hard, for his pranks are funny and if someone is going to play jokes on me, I'd rather it be one of my childhood heroes than anyone else.

225

KANE HODDER
MASTER TATTOO ARTIST

During my year with Kane I have seen over a dozen people with Kane's autograph tattooed on their body, hell, there has even been a 60-year-old woman who got one! So while we were at the tattoo convention I was not shocked when three different people came up to Kane, got him to sign their bodies and then had it tattooed on them. Though this was the first time I got to see it in action.

Having never even seen someone get a tattoo in person, it was almost an overload to my brain seeing hundreds of people everywhere getting them done. The entire ballroom was filled with a constant buzzing of flesh being marked forever. Getting to stand close to people and watch Kane's name going on a man's arm for the rest of their life was interesting to say the least. We interviewed one of them as they got it done, when we asked him why the tattoo, he just said, *because Kane is badass.* And he is right; Kane is, though I still could never imagine getting anyone's name tattooed on my body!

The funny thing is, I think if someone tattooed my name on their body, I'd feel like I'd owe them something. Like they were then my property and I had to take care of them, like I branded a cow. I'd probably check in with them every week, make sure they are all right and see if they need anything.

Before I headed down that weekend, I put up a post on Facebook asking for a volunteer to have Kane tattoo them. Kane has always wanted to actually tattoo a person himself... what a better opportunity than at a convention for them? Within a few minutes of the post, we had a brave volunteer respond... Colin Foster. The man said he would do it; I was excited because we wanted to get this on film for our reality show pitch. Since he said he would, I just figured he probably had fifty tattoos already... little did I know Colin had NO tattoos; it would be his first.

Colin arrived early with his father for some support. All of us talked and joked for a while as we waited for the artists to clear their booth to let us in. During this time, I noticed a button on the wall next to Kane's booth. Two green buttons, one said *on*, the other *off*. I nudged Kane and said, I wonder what they did. Standing up, Kane, Colin and I looked at it and figured it would just shut off a few lights. Of course, Kane pushed it. At first, nothing happened and I shrugged my shoulder... then like a dimmer light, ALL the power in the ballroom went out. The dozens of buzzing tattoo pens suddenly shut off in mid-tattoo. I started laughing so hard I almost fell to the floor; Kane on the other hand flicked it back on and acted like nothing happened. Thankfully, we happened to get that on camera... though I do feel bad for all the people who now have a smudge on their tattoo.

Kane Concentrating on the Tattoo

After a long wait, the Hornet's Nest Tattooing was ready for us. At this point, Kane was tired and not sure he even wanted to do it, though I think that was the nerves talking. Colin on the other hand, put on a brave face, though he did request I get him a shot from the booth next door so he could settle his nerves. Within seconds of Kane and Colin sitting

228

down, a giant crowed grew to watch Kane give his first tattoo. The artist in the booth walked Kane through the steps, put the stencil on Colin's leg and let him at it. Amazingly, Kane wasn't that bad and Colin took the pain like a man. I on the other hand was cringing the whole time, waiting for Kane to slip and puncture Colin's leg or mess up that tat forever. Instead, almost thirty minutes later, Kane had put a cute little Jason mask and his initials on Colin's leg forever.

 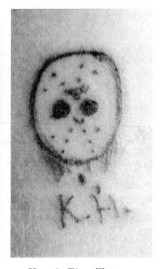

Colin Foster…Brave Man **Kane's First Tattoo**

After some pictures in the booth and of the tattoo, Colin's leg was wrapped up and he was ready to head into his new life as a man tattooed by a film legend. Pretty damn cool if you ask me.

229

Michael Aloisi

THE END... IS JUST THE BEGINNING

As I sit and write this now, there is only a month until the release of Kane's biography and this book you are reading. With the release and the book tour so close, I am panicking to say the least... especially since I'm behind on handing this in! Though obviously, if you are reading this, I succeeded.

Closing out this journal that I have been writing for... wow, that is odd, exactly 13 months, I feel a bit sad that it has to end. Though at the same time, this is really just the very beginning of The Killer and I. Over the past year, I spent close to a dozen weekends with Kane, and those dozen weekends gave me enough experiences to write an entire book! And now I'm about to set out on the road with him for three months straight. I can't imagine the amount of stories I will have from the tour. Hopefully you'll be getting to not only read those entries online and in another book, but that you'll also get to watch them on our television show. As of now we are extremely close to getting a deal for it to be produced, but who knows, it could all fall through. Regardless if we get the show or not, I will always have these experiences with Kane and the ones that will happen in the coming months.

Thank you for reading this book and following me on my journey. I hope you'll keep reading along as Kane leads me down the path to hell.

The Killer and I

ACKNOWLEDGMENTS

I believe I have thanked everyone I wanted to in the back of Kane's biography, but I guess a few more can be done here. A huge thank you to my wife for believing in every single crazy idea I have ever come up with. Without her undying support, I would not be heading out on the road to do a national book tour with one of my childhood idols. I love her more than I can explain in words.

Again, thank you to my parents and brother for helping me throughout my life.

Thank you to Gina Petrone for editing this book (which is equivalent to cutting through a rain forest with nail clippers) and being a good friend.

Thank you to Amanda Loveless of Loveless FX for doing a bloody good make-up job for the cover of this book and the publicity photos.

Lastly, I guess I have to do it, a HUGE thanks to Kane Hodder. He took a chance on a small time author and publishing company and changed my life forever. I'm honored to have worked with him for the last year and to be setting out on the road to promote our books. As much as he drives me nuts, he is a great guy and I'll forever be grateful to him.

CPSIA information can be obtained at www.ICGtesting.com
Printed in the USA
BVOW02s0049061115

425933BV00001B/1/P